THE
WORLD
ACCORDING
TO
RUMMY

The
WORLD
ACCORDING
TO
RUMMY

WARNING: This book is not authorized, endorsed or approved by Donald H. Rumsfeld

Welcome Rain Publishers
New York

The World According to Rummy

Manufactured in the United States of America.

Library of Congress Cataloging-in-Publication Data is available.

ISBN 1-55649-950-X

CONTENTS

EDITOR'S NOTE

What follows is by no means an attempt to present the world as Mr. Rumsfeld sees it; it is an effort to illustrate those particular aspects of his worldview that are at odds with reality as it is percieved by most reasonable people.

Ironically, it is his own words—and those of his admirers that provide the key to understanding where Rummy has gone so terribly wrong.

The reader with a keen sense of irony (a weapon curiously missing from Mr. Rumsfeld's otherwise impressive intellectual arsenal) will here find that the very same traits that have made Rummy a hero to some lead others to think of him as an arrogant bully who personifies the callousness and drive for world domination that are hallmarks of the Bush administration.

It never occurs to Mr. Rumsfeld that his my way or the highway, winner take all, it has nothing to do with oil, diplomacy is for wimps persona might nourish the very resentments that lead to terrorism. Or that not everyone would agree that when terrorists kill innocent people it's murder; but when the United States government kills a lot more innocent people, it's "collateral damage." When Mr. Rumsfeld talks about the liars whose regimes we will change, he seems to be oblivious to the fact that many Americans have noticed that we have been lied to—by our own government.

He thinks that when the U.S. attacks its own allies in Afghanistan and they fire back, we have the right to kill them in "self-defense." He's against the draft, but has no problem with a "stop loss" program that keeps as many as 30,000 service people in action for up to 16 months beyond their tour of duty.

As Secretary of Offense, Mr. Rumsfeld has cast a Fog of Language over the members of the press corps, frequently belittling them for errors in grammar and the inelegant construction of their questions. He is careful to quote the C.I.A. or the president, Dr. Rice or his good friend Colin Powell whenever talking about WMD or the tight relationship between Iraq and al Qaeda—enabling him to say "I never said that, I was just repeating what so-and-so said" when caught out. When asked how it was possible for the Department of Defense not to know that planes might be used as a weapon—given ample precedent, he clarified: "Well, I didn't say we didn't know. I said I didn't know." Mr. Rumsfeld is a master of misdirection through false precision.

The events of 9/11 challenged America to redefine itself in the world. As Sir John Keegan wrote in his article about Rummy in *Vanity Fair*, "Terrorism in the name of Islam is, fundamentally, an idea. Only a cleverer and more flexible idea will defeat it." If the best idea Mr. Rumsfeld has been able to come up with is kill them all (or detain them indefinitely), then we are in real trouble, because the Bush administration is not exactly rife with people with clever or flexible ideas.

If America's chief exports during the Bush administration are weapons, greed, fear, hypocrisy, and death instead of freedom, equality, democracy, and opportunity, there is no defense strategy or budget—hundreds of billions or even a trillion dollars—that can protect us from reaping what we are sowing.

—John Weber

THE
WORLD
ACCORDING
TO
RUMMY

THE WORLD
IS A
DANGEROUS PLACE

RUMSFELD: There's no question but that we live in a danger-ous and untidy world.

—DoD News Briefing, May 30/02

I think that we're unlikely to be successful in changing the nature of human beings. That's for others. What we need to do is to recognize that we live in a world that's a dangerous world, it's an untidy world, it's a big world. We have to engage in that world as free people, because the linkages we have across this globe are so centrally a part of our lives, as to how we live our lives, that we have no choice but to contribute to a more peaceful and stable world.

—DoD News Briefing, September 20/01

Concerning the need for elegant intelligence . . .

Mr. Rumsfeld's remarks drew several pointed questions from the audience challenging how the administration could defend its doctrine of preemptive strikes against perceived threats when the precise intelligence needed for such a strategy appar-ently failed in the case of Iraq.

"If you're going to live in this world, and it is a dangerous world, you have to have elegant intelligence," Mr. Rumsfeld acknowledged.

—*The New York Times*, February 4/04

I'm struck by the fact that at Dick Cheney's confirmation hearings in 1989 not a single senator asked him about Iraq. The word never came up. And a year later we're at war with Iraq in the Persian Gulf. It made me wonder what word, what name of a country or what word for a military capability wasn't mentioned in my confirmation hearing four months ago that within a year could come up and dominate our lives.

—Interview with Jim Garamone,
American Forces Information Service, May 29/01

[Rumsfeld] routinely handed out or recommended a book called *Pearl Harbor: Warning and Decision* by Roberta Wohlstetter. Rumsfeld particularly recommended the foreword, written by Thomas Schelling, who argued that Pearl Harbor was an ordinary blunder, the type government specializes in. "There is a tendency in our planning to confuse the unfamiliar with the improbable. . . . The danger is in a poverty of expectations, a routine obsession with a few dangers that may be familiar rather than likely."

—Bob Woodward, *Bush at War*
(New York: Simon & Schuster, 2002), pp. 22–3

Visit with your predecessors from various administrations. They know the ropes and can help you see around some corners. Try to make original mistakes, rather than needlessly repeating theirs.

—from "Rumsfeld's Rules"*

---

*This admonition is from "Rumsfeld's Rules," written in 1974, copyright in 1980 and revised on September 10, 2001. The entire document is available on the web.

In his testimony, Mr Rumsfeld told commission members that he considered al Qaeda a serious threat before Sept. 11 and that he had been taking steps to prepare the military to combat terrorism . . .

But the report prepared by the commission staff portrayed Mr. Rumsfeld as a new secretary struggling with getting his senior aides into place and focused on other priorities, like missile defenses.

Mr. Rumsfeld, for instance, never received a briefing from the Pentagon's departing senior counterterrorism expert, the report noted, and counterterrorism aides said "the new team was focused on other issues and was not especially interested in the counterterrorism agenda."

In interviews with commission staff members, Mr. Rumsfeld "did not recall any particular counterterrorism issue that engaged his attention before 9/11," the report said.

—*The New York Times*, March 24/04

RUSSERT: Did you ever imagine that, as the Secretary of Defense, that your building, the Pentagon, would be attacked by a terrorist using an American commercial airline?

RUMSFELD: Oh, goodness no. Never would have crossed anyone's mind that a commercial airline—usually a hijacker who takes an airplane, of course, wants to get someplace or wants to make a statement or wants to go on television or wants to hold hostages, but this is a distinctly different behavior pattern than we've seen previously, and now, obviously, it's something we have to be attentive to.

—Interview on NBC *Meet the Press*
with Tim Russert, September 30/01

RATHER: As regards the attacks of September 11th, was it, in your opinion, a failure of intelligence or a failure of imagination?

RUMSFELD: If you know anyone whose imagination was sufficient to think of plastic knives and the use of a U.S. airliner filled with American people as a missile to destroy a World Trade Center before it happened, I'd be amazed.

—Interview with Dan Rather, CBS, October 9/01

RUMSFELD: First I must say, I knew of no intelligence during the six-plus months leading up to September 11th that indicated terrorists would hijack commercial airliners, use them as missiles to fly into the Pentagon or the World Trade Center towers . . .

KERREY: . . . .You said you received no specific intelligence about the possibility of a plane being used as a bomb. Mr. Secretary, you're well known as somebody who thinks about all kinds of terrible possibilities that might happen that nobody else is thinking about. I mean, that's what you do so well when you're going into a difficult situation. . . . Let me put it this way to you. Let's say that the Federal Aviation Administration had heeded some warnings about the possibility of a hijacking and had altered the procedures in American airports to prevent these hijackers from being able to get on the planes in the first place; or had different procedures on the airports on the morning of 11th of September to make certain the pilots were locked up front and that the passengers didn't remain in their seats and cooperate. (Applause.) Let's say that 9/11 hadn't happened. Would you have gone to the American people and carried out the strategy that you say you worked on all year long and came up with on the 4th of September? Because the president had to go to the American people and said, we're going to work to eliminate the al Qaeda network, we're going to use all national elements of the power to do so, diplomatic, military, economic, intel, information, law enforcement. And we're going to eliminate sanctions for al Qaeda and related terrorist networks. And if diplomatic efforts fail to do so, we're going to consider additional measures. Earlier in your testimony, you said all the reasons why to do such a thing would provoke angry response. Would the administration have put this policy in place were it not for 9/11?

RUMSFELD: I believe we would have. One can't announce that for certainty, because 9/11 happened. But it had been worked on, developed and was ready to go into place . . .

KERREY: I've got to say, Mr. Secretary, if that's the case—and I trust you, I believe you on this point—then I don't think it's a good argument to say that the American people wouldn't have accepted something prior to 9/11 that was unpopular, because you just said that absent 9/11 you would have recommended to the president to put in place a policy that would have been exceptionally unpopular and difficult to sell. I believe he should have, by the way, regardless of whether or not 9/11 happened. But it doesn't work. The argument falls on its face if you say, Please understand, we couldn't have done this before 9/11, if you say you would have done it absent 9/11.

RUMSFELD: I understand.

—Public Testimony Before 9/11 Panel, March 23/04

BEN-VENISTE: With respect to your comment about domestic intelligence and what we knew as of September 10th, 2001, your statement was that you knew of no intelligence to suggest that planes would be hijacked in the United States and flown into buildings. Well, it is correct that the United States intelligence community had a great deal of intelligence suggesting that the terrorists, back since 1994, had plans, discussed plans, to use airplanes as weapons, loaded with fuel, loaded with bombs, loaded with explosives. The Algerians had a plan in '94 to fly a plane into the Eiffel Tower. The Bojinka plot in '95 discussed flying an explosive-laden small plane into CIA headquarters. Certainly CIA was well aware of that. There were plans in '97 using a UAV. In '98, an al Qaeda-connected group talked about flying a commercial plane into the World Trade Center. In '98, there was a plot broken up by Turkish intelligence involving the use of a plane as a weapon. In '99, there was a plot involving exploding a plane at an airport. Also in '99, there was a plot regarding an explosive-laden hang glider. In '99 or in 2000, there was a plot regarding hijacking a 747. And in August of 2001, there was information . . . received by our intelligence community regarding flying a plane into the Nairobi embassy, our Nairobi embassy. And so I suggest that when you have this threat spike in the summer of 2001 that said something huge was going to happen and the FAA circulates, as you mentioned, a warning which does nothing to alert people on the ground to the potential threat of jihadist hijacking, which only, it seems to me, despite the fact that they read into the congressional record the potential for a hijacking threat in the United States, in the summer of 2001, it never gets to any actionable level. Nobody at the airports is alerted to any particular threat. Nobody flying the planes takes action of a defensive posture. I understand that going after al Qaeda overseas is one thing. But protecting the United States is another thing. And it seems to me that a statement that we could not conceive of such a thing happening really does not reflect the state of our intelligence community as of 2001, sir.

RUMSFELD: A couple of comments. I quite agree with you, there were a number of reports about potential hijacking. I even remember comments about UAVs. I even have seen things about private aircraft hitting something. But I do not recall ever seeing anything in the period since I came back to government about the idea of taking a commercial airliner and using it as a missile. I just don't recall seeing it . . .

BEN-VENISTE: Let me just follow it up briefly to say that we knew that terrorists had attacked us in '93 at the World Trade Center. We knew in the millennium plot in December of '99 that al Qaeda had an operative sleeper in the United States, or coming to the United States, who planned to blow up LAX. That was interdicted. They were on high alert during the millennium plot, and they thought about domestic terrorism in that regard. And now, as we get into 2001, it just seems to me

like we're looking at the white truck that had everyone capti-
vated during the hunt for the sniper. Everybody was looking in
the wrong direction. Why weren't people thinking about protecting the United States? We knew that there were two al
Qaeda operatives in the United States. And yet that information does not get circulated. It doesn't get to the people at the
airports. It doesn't go on Most Wanted on television where
people could identify such individuals. We know that a man
named Moussaoui has been identified as somebody who took
lessons on just how to steer an airplane, not how to take it off,
not how to land it, just how to steer it. So it seems to me when
you make the statement, sir, that we didn't know that planes
might be used as weapons in the summer of 2001, I just have
to take issue with that.

RUMSFELD: Well, I didn't say we didn't know. I said I didn't
know. . . .

—Public Testimony Before 9/11 Panel, March 23/04

It means we are good at intelligence.

Anyone with an ounce of sense can look back at the intelligence and find out that from the time something began until
we figured it out, in dozens of cases it took two, four, six, eight,
10, 12, in one case 13 years, and I was informed today that
there may be one that's 17 years, between the time it happened
and the time we found out about it. Does that mean we're not
good at intelligence? No, it doesn't. It means we are good at
intelligence. It just means it's a very tough world we live in.
And it's a very complicated world. And we have to expect that
whatever comes out on an agency piece of paper with an
agreed-upon community opinion and assessment, that it is
based on what they know. And it is not based on what they
know they don't know, and it's not based on what they don't
know they don't know. Therefore one has to assume that this
is the least of it.

—DoD News Briefing, October 17/02

The military, which seemed to have contingency plans for the most inconceivable scenarios, had no plans for Afghanistan, the sanctuary of bin Laden and his network.

—Woodward, *Bush at War*, p. 25

We are encouraged bin Laden is not as clever as people have given him credit for . . .

LEHRER: Do you feel like you're against a smart enemy, a lucky enemy, a fanatic? How do you characterize them?

RUMSFELD: Well, certainly, a large fraction of the ones that are left have to be of the bin Laden type, attitudinally, philosophically. And if you watch some of the tapes he's made and read some of his comments, it's chilling. I mean this is a man who rules everyone out who doesn't agree with him. And he's willing to kill as many tens of thousands of people as he's able to find.

—Interview with Jim Lehrer
for *PBS NewsHour*, November 7/01

HUME: Let's turn to the question of chemical and biological weapons. One of these peculiar statements that emanates from al Qaeda, presumably from bin Laden himself, says he's got chemical and biological and nuclear weapons. What is your take on that?

RUMSFELD: Well, he is a person who I am relieved to find out is accident-prone. He's made mistakes lately. He's made statements that have been very harmful to his cause.

SNOW: How so?

HUME: What are you talking about?

RUMSFELD: Well, he's—first he attacks the United Nations and lumps every country in the world that is associated as being outside of the acceptable range of behavior. Then he discusses his access to chemical, biological and nuclear or radiation weapons. I'm encouraged that he apparently is feeling a lot of pressure and is not as clever as people have given him credit for.

—Interview with Tony Snow and Brit Hume,
Fox News Sunday, November 11/01

RAINES: I'm going to leave it to the experts to ask the difficult questions and I'll ask the easy one, which is . . . bin Laden's whereabouts and how close we are to him.

RUMSFELD: I've tried to say this in a way that is understandable, but—and the only thing I could figure out is if you're chasing the chicken around the chicken yard and you don't have him yet. And the question is how close are you? The answer is it's tough to characterize because there's lots of zigs and zags.

—Meeting with the editorial board
of *The New York Times*, November 14/01

Q: Mr. Secretary, the Afghan Defense Ministry said today that bin Laden had escaped to Pakistan and was being protected by an Islamic militant leader. Do you have any reason to believe that he may have gotten out of Afghanistan? How important is it now to the success of the operation that he be found dead or alive?

RUMSFELD: We hear six, seven, eight 10, 12 conflicting reports every day. I've stopped chasing them. We do know, of certain knowledge, that he is either in Afghanistan or in some other country or dead.

—DoD News Briefing, December 27/01

Do not misconstrue or mischaracterize the work
of the clean-up man . . .

Q: . . . There were strikes in Kandahar and Kabul and there's talk about the electricity system going down. Are you running the risk of being characterized as attacking the Afghan people rather than military targets?

RUMSFELD: You know, in this world of ours, if you get up in the morning you're running a risk of having someone lie and someone mischaracterize what it is you're doing.

—DoD News Briefing, October 7/01

Evidence is for wimps.

Q: What do you make of the statement made by the Iraqi government yesterday that Iraq has no weapons of mass destruction and is not developing any?

RUMSFELD: They are lying. Next.

—Media availability at Kuwait City International Airport,
Kuwait City, Kuwait, June 10/02

Q: When you say that Iraq is lying. That story mentioned having weapons—

RUMSFELD: Sometimes I understate for emphasis.

Q: I don't think I missed the point. But it was a two-part thing, that they were not developing and that they did not have any. Were they lying about one, or both?

RUMSFELD: No. They have them and they continue to develop them and they have weaponized chemical weapons, we know that. They've had an active program to develop nuclear weapons. It's also clear that they are actively developing biological weapons. I don't know what other kinds of weapons would fall under the rubric of weapons of mass destruction, but if there are more, I suspect they're working on them as well, even though I don't happen to know what they are. It is just false, not true, inaccurate and typical.

—Media availability at Kuwait City International Airport,
Kuwait City, Kuwait, June 10/02

"All you have to do is read the newspaper."

Q: On Iraq, sir, one of the things our partners in the international community are apparently interested in is evidence of Iraq's intentions, particularly with weapons of mass destruction. Before they make a decision as to what they might or might not do, do you have fresh evidence that you can make public now on Iraq's intentions with weapons of mass destruction? . . .

RUMSFELD: I thought the President laid out the . . . public case very very well. . . .When I hear the word evidence it conjures up a couple of things for me. One is that somebody is misguided and is looking for the kind of information that you could take into a court of law and prove beyond a reasonable doubt and that's one mind-set kind of under Article 3 of our Constitution in the criminal justice system where the goal is to punish a person, which of course the goal is not here to punish anybody. The goal is to learn information and to have them disarm themselves of their weapons of mass destruction capabilities. There's no debate in the world as to whether they have those weapons. There's no debate in the world as to whether they're continuing to develop and acquire them. There's no debate in the world as to whether or not he's used them. There's no debate in the world as to whether or not he's consistently threatening his neighbors with them. We all know that. A trained ape knows that. All you have to do is read the newspaper.

—Media Roundtable, September 13/02

We have elegant intelligence on
the relationship between Iraq and al Qaeda . . .

Q: . . . what kind of evidence is there that the government of Iraq is any way hosting, supporting, sponsoring al Qaeda or any other terrorists inside Iraq?

RUMSFELD: Well, I suppose that at some moment, it may make sense to discuss that publicly. It doesn't today. But what I have said is a fact—that there are al Qaeda in a number of locations in Iraq. And the suggestion that those people who are so attentive in denying human rights to their population aren't aware of where these folks are or what they're doing is ludicrous.

—DoD News Briefing, August 20/02

Q: Mr. Secretary, Condi Rice was interviewed on television last night and she said that . . . al Qaeda had—I believe she put it, "taken refuge" in Baghdad. And she also said that suspect al Qaeda captives had told the United States that al Qaeda has been trained by Iraq in how to make chemical weapons. Could you shed any light on either of those, including whether or not these al Qaeda in Baghdad might be senior al Qaeda?

RUMSFELD: The knowledge that the intelligence community, the shared intelligence information among the coalition members, has of the al Qaeda relationship with Iraq is evolving. It's based on a lot of different types of sources of varying degrees of reliability. Some of it, admittedly, comes from detainees, which has been helpful, and particularly some high-ranking detainees. Since we began after September 11th, we do have solid evidence of the presence in Iraq of al Qaeda members, including some that have been in Baghdad. We have what we consider to be very reliable reporting of senior level contacts going back a decade, and of possible chemical and biological agent training. And when I say contacts, I mean between Iraq and al Qaeda. The reports of these contacts have been increas-

ing since 1998. We have what we believe to be credible information that Iraq and al Qaeda have discussed safe haven
opportunities in Iraq, reciprocal nonaggression discussions. We
have what we consider to be credible evidence that al Qaeda
leaders have sought contacts in Iraq who could help them
acquire weapon of—weapons of mass destruction capabilities.
We do have—I believe it's one report indicating that Iraq provided unspecified training relating to chemical and/or biological matters for al Qaeda members. There is, I'm told, also some
other information of varying degrees of reliability that supports
that conclusion of their cooperation.

—DoD News Briefing, September 26/02

Q: Earlier this week you came out and said there's a link
between Baghdad and al Qaeda. This report [inaudible] came
from prisoners, a lot of the intelligence reporting came from
prisoners. How credible was this information?

RUMSFELD: I wouldn't have said if it were not totally credible.

Q: So there's a link in your mind.

RUMSFELD: Not in my mind, from the ground. It's in fact. It's
just that simple.

—Interview with Dan Ronan, Fox Affiliate – WAGA
Channel 5, Atlanta, Ga., September 27/02

***Who's he talking about: a) Osama bin Laden;
b) Saddam Hussein; or c) George W. Bush?***

I mean everyone builds their own reputation and they have to
live with it. And if someone's a liar in politics, you all pin the
tail on the donkey and pretty soon people assume that that
person may or may not be telling the truth.

—Meeting with the editorial board
of *The New York Times*, November 14/01

Absence of evidence is not evidence of absence . . .

KROFT: U.N. weapons inspectors are preparing to go to Iraq very shortly and begin searching for evidence of Saddam Hussein's weapons of mass destruction. What do you expect them to find, and what happens if they don't find anything? Is Saddam Hussein off the hook?

RUMSFELD: Well, we know that Saddam Hussein has chemical and biological weapons. And we know he has an active program for the development of nuclear weapons. I suppose what it would prove would be that the inspections process had been successfully defeated by the Iraqis if they find nothing. That's what one would know if that turned out to be the case.

— Interview with Steve Kroft,
Infinity Radio, November 14/02

RUMSFELD: The responsibility under the resolutions for disarming and for proving that Iraq has disarmed and has no weapons of mass destruction any more—we certainly know they did, right? The inspectors found these things after a defector told them where to go. And they found active programs. So, we know they did. So, let's pretend they don't today. The responsibility for demonstrating that is . . . on Iraq. And it's important to get that into one's mind, because it is Iraq that is the subject of the resolutions, and the resolutions call for them to be open and demonstrate that they have disarmed, and no longer have any of those programs which they did—

Q: Mr. Secretary—

RUMSFELD: —and we know they do.

Q: —let's pretend that they do, and you have evidence that they do.

RUMSFELD: We don't have to pretend they do, Charlie.

Q: Well—

RUMSFELD: They do.

—DoD News Briefing, December 3/02

RUMSFELD: Good afternoon. After United Nations (U.N.) inspectors briefed the Security Council last week, a number of the observers seemed to seize on the inspectors' statement that they found "no smoking gun" as yet. Conversely, if the inspectors had found new evidence, the argument might then have been that inspections were in fact working and, therefore, they should be given more time to work. I guess for any who are unalterably opposed to military action, no matter what Iraq may do, there will be some sort of an argument. Another way to look at it is this; that the fact that the inspectors have not yet come up with new evidence of Iraq's WMD program could be evidence in and of itself of Iraq's non-cooperation. We do know that Iraq has designed its programs in a way that they can proceed in an environment of inspections, and that they are skilled at denial and deception.

—DoD News Briefing, January 15/03

Don't blame the boss. He has enough problems.

—from "Rumsfeld's Rules"

Q: . . . do you have evidence that they currently have them [that Iraq currently has WMD], or are you just basing it on the fact that they had them?

RUMSFELD: It—I do not think that if it were the latter, the president would be saying what he's saying or the director of Central Intelligence would be saying what he's saying.

—DoD News Briefing, January 7/03

Q: But as you see it now, do you believe that Iraq does present an imminent danger, imminent threat?

RUMSFELD: The President has stated—our job here is to be prepared to do what we're asked. The President has stated that he considers the Saddam Hussein regime a danger to the United States and a danger to the region; that it has weapons of mass destruction, that it is developing still more, and that it has linkages to terrorist activities; and that every other effort has been exhausted—the diplomatic, the economic, limited military activity in the Northern and Southern low—no-fly zones; and that the string is running out.

—DoD News Briefing, January 29/03

Who are you going to believe, Secretary Powell or Saddam Hussein?

Q: Mr. Secretary, today in a broadcast interview, Saddam Hussein said, "There is only one truth: Iraq has no weapons of mass destruction whatsoever." And he went on to say, "I would like to tell you directly we have no relationship with al Qaeda."

RUMSFELD: And Abraham Lincoln was short.

Q: Would you care to respond directly to what Saddam Hussein has said today?

RUMSFELD: How does one respond to that? I mean, he said that Secretary Powell's words tomorrow are going to be lies. He says that the photographs that will be shown will be doctored. That's what he does. That's what he does. And then the world's press spreads it around the world as though it's true. It's utter — it's just a continuous pattern. This is a case of the local liar coming up again and people repeating what he said and forgetting to say that he never—almost never—rarely tells the truth.

—DoD News Briefing, February 4/03

We're still waiting . . .

Q: But don't you believe if the American people are about to commit their sons and daughters to a war against Iraq, that in order to make that decision, the American people have the right to know these facts?

RUMSFELD: They certainly ought to have as much information as can possibly be given, and they will.

—DoD News Briefing, January 29/03

It is unquestionably about the
weapons of mass destruction . . .

AL JAZEERA: I would like to put it to you straight away the issue between you, the Bush administration, and Iraq is not weapons of mass destruction. It is for you—how to get rid of Saddam Hussein and his regime.

RUMSFELD: Well, wrong. It is about weapons of mass destruction. It is unquestionably about that.

—Interview with Jamil Azer, Al Jazeera TV, February 25/03

Where are the Weapons of Mass Destruction?
You just need to know where to look:

STEPHANOPOULOS: Finally, weapons of mass destruction. Key goal of the military campaign is finding those weapons of mass destruction. None have been found yet. There was a raid on the Answar Al-Islam Camp up in the north last night. A lot of people expected to find ricin there. None was found. How big of a problem is that? And is it curious to you that given how much control U.S. and coalition forces now have in the country, they haven't found any weapons of mass destruction?

RUMSFELD: Not at all. If you think—let me take that, both pieces—the area in the south and the west and the north that coalition forces control is substantial. It happens not to be the area where weapons of mass destruction were dispersed. We know where they are. They're in the area around Tikrit and Baghdad and east, west, south and north somewhat.

—Interview on ABC *This Week*
with George Stephanopoulos, March 30/03

RUSSERT: Let me turn to the whole idea of and issue of weapons of mass destruction. George Will, conservative commentator who supported the war, wrote this column, and let me read it to you and our viewers, because it's very important: "Some say the war was justified even if weapons of mass destruction are not found nor their destruction explained, because the world is better off without Saddam Hussein. Of course it is better off. But unless one is prepared to postulate a U.S. right, perhaps even a duty, to militarily dismantle any tyranny, it is unacceptable to argue that Hussein's mass graves and torture chambers suffice as retrospective justifications for preemptive war. Americans seem sanguine about the failure—so far—to validate the war's premise about the threat posed by Hussein's weapons of mass destruction. But a long-term failure would unravel much of this president's policy and rhetoric." If we don't find the weapons of mass destruction, will the president, will our country's credibility, be hurt severely?

RUMSFELD: I think we will find them. And why do I say that? I say that because I have got confidence in our intelligence community and the intelligence communities in other countries.

RUSSERT: In March you did say, quote, "We know where they are."

—Interview on NBC *Meet the Press*
with Tim Russert, July 13/03

Q: But, you have to admit, the major reason to justify the war . . . was because of the stockpiles of weapons of mass destruction.

RUMSFELD: Indeed, that's why the Congress passed the resolution, that's why the United Nations passed its resolution, and that's why there was unanimous agreement, not about whether or not he had filed a fraudulent declaration, but the only question was about timing, whether it should be done here, or later, after still another resolution.

—Interview with Wolf Blitzer, CNN, March 14/04

Who's he talking about: a) Saddam Hussein; b) George W. Bush; c) himself?

You know, in life, if a person doesn't tell the truth, those people who become aware of that know it. They—suddenly, they're aware of it, and they tell other people. And that individual who doesn't tell the truth pays a penalty. He pays a penalty in a company, pays a penalty in a city or a town, in an industry, in a unit. There's a punishment; there's a penalty, as there should be, for a person who makes a practice of not telling the truth. It's interesting to me that a government that consistently does not tell the truth seems not to pay a penalty. Everything they say is accepted. Everything they say is repeated. Everything they say, notwithstanding the fact that they have lied over and over and over again, and yet there it comes: "They said this. What do you think about this?"

—DoD News Briefing, September 30/02

Q: Is the U.S. in any way exaggerating or misleading the American public in regard to the potential threat posed by Iraq, as charged by these [members of congress]—

RUMSFELD: Is the U.S. government—you mean the senior members of the administration?

Q: Correct.

RUMSFELD: Not to my knowledge. And if I knew of an instance, I would certainly correct it.

—DoD News Briefing, September 30/02

***Without revealing anything, you can rest assured
that we have elegant intelligence on
Pakistan's nuclear program . . .***

The countries that have nuclear weapons have spent a good deal of time getting them and a good deal of time thinking about them and a good deal of time thinking about why they have them. And if there's anything . . . that people become aware of, it's that those weapons are enormously dangerous and enormously lethal. The risk of not handling them well is so great that you must in fact take every conceivable step to assure to their safety and their reliability and their protection. I have every confidence that Pakistan will do that.

—Media stakeout at Fox and CBS studios,
Washington, D.C., November 11/01

Q: Sir, on India and Pakistan, as far as we know President Musharraf does not have final control over nuclear weapons and it's in the hands of the military. Is that something that concerns you?

RUMSFELD: I think you better check your facts.

Q: Does that mean he does actually have—?

RUMSFELD: I think you better check your facts. I think the premise of your question ought to be checked.

Q: Do you believe he has control over the nuclear arsenal?

RUMSFELD: I think, without revealing anything, I think intelligent people can make a reasonable assumption that leaders of countries with nuclear weapons are not inattentive to the management of those weapons.

—Media availability en route to Tallinn, Estonia, June 7/02

Let's not over-think this . . .

You have two choices. If you see puddling or pools of these people gathering through your intel, and then you've got a choice, how do you feel about that? Do you want a collection of terrorists who wish you ill to just sit there and puddle and go about their business killing neighboring people, or not? And the [answer is]—if you [do]—then you don't do anything. If you do something, you're going to find them and capture them or kill them . . . and it seems to me it's a no-brainer. It's a three-minute decision. The first two are for coffee.

—DoD News Briefing, June 18/03

Point of clarification:

RUSSERT: Robert Byrd, the Democratic senator from West Virginia, said [Iraq is] an urban guerrilla shooting gallery.

RUMSFELD: I heard that.

RUSSERT: Do you agree?

RUMSFELD: Well, it is not restricted to urban areas, for one thing. It is happening in some urban centers. It is also happening in some non-urban areas. . . .

—Interview on NBC *Meet the Press*
with Tim Russert, July 13/03

Invest in never-ending war:

We were talking last night, a few of us, about comparing this effort to a war, and it undoubtedly will prove to be a lot more like a cold war than a hot war, in this sense. If you think about it, in the Cold War it took 50 years, plus or minus. It did not involve major battles. It involved continuous pressure. It involved cooperation by a host of nations. It involved the willingness of populations in many countries to invest in it and to sustain it. It took leadership at the top from a number of countries that were willing to be principled and to be courageous and to put things at risk; and when it ended, it ended not with a bang, but through internal collapse. The support for that way of life and that pressure against the world and that threat to the world—just disintegrated from inside. And it's just by accident, and in discussing this with some people that it strikes me that that might be a more appropriate way to think about what we are up against here, than would be any major conflict.

—Secretary Rumsfeld media availability
with traveling press, Cairo, Egypt, October 4/01

Q: Sir, what constitutes a victory in this new environment?

A: . . . Now, what is victory? I say that victory is persuading the American people and the rest of the world that this is not a quick matter that's going to be over in a month or a year or even five years. It is something that we need to do so that we can continue to live in a world with powerful weapons and with people who are willing to use those powerful weapons. And we can do that as a country. And that would be a victory, in my view.

—DoD News Briefing, September 20/01

REMEMBER WHERE
YOU CAME FROM*

It's an all-or-nothing world . . .

The consensus among many of Rumsfeld's friends is that the
role he has come to play is somehow connected to his qualities and experiences as a wrestler. A champion wrestler,
they explain, is someone who is always in condition for combat, who knows that he is solely responsible for the outcome
of his battles, and whose victories . . . are by their very
nature winner-take-all.

—Midge Decter, *Rumsfeld*
(New York: HarperCollins, 2003), p. 215

The Rumsfeld family spent the ambassador's free time traveling
around, sometimes meeting up—as they would continue all
through their lives to do—with old friends from America. One
of these reunions . . . included a visit to Pamplona to witness the
famous running of the bulls. . . . Don [was] unable to resist the
call of adventure. . . . As the bulls came thundering down the
street in the direction of the building from which they were
watching, they saw him running along with the crowd of young

---

*from "Rumsfeld's Rules"

blades who turn up each year and then test their mettle in eluding the animals' growing rage. And just as the bulls were within hot-breath range of the forty-one-year-old foreign dignitary, he leapt up, grabbed hold of a lamppost, and hung there until the stampede passed. (As more and more people would come to discover over the years, it is no easy thing—even for a bull—to win out with someone who is always at the ready for a testing.)

—Decter, *Rumsfeld*, pp. 60–61

Q: . . . your dad, generally, what did he teach you about life?

RUMSFELD: He was a voracious reader, and certainly that was an important learning experience for me to see— My mother was a schoolteacher and he was a person who loved to read, mostly history and biographies. That had an effect on me. He was very energetic. He loved life. I remember him whistling all the time and he was upbeat. And he liked people and he liked doing things and he would go out, he started working at a real estate firm when he was, I think, 12 or 13, as an office boy. Part time. But when I was a young kid and I would caddy at golf, he never had time to play golf because he worked day and night, seven days a week, but he would go out and play golf, nine holes at dusk, in about 35 minutes. He never took a warm-up stroke. He would just get on that course and hit the ball and go, and hit the ball and go. It was so much fun to be with him.

—Interview with Rowan Scarborough, October 18/03

A second chance . . .

To manage twenty-first-century military preparedness and geopolitics, the Bush administration reached back to the final years of the Vietnam War. Donald Rumsfeld and Richard Cheney, as chief of staff and deputy chief of staff, respectively, had presided over the machinery of the Ford

White House in the spring of 1975. This was the bitter April when Saigon finally fell to the North Vietnamese, followed several weeks later by the mishandling of the rescue of the SS *Mayaguez*, an American merchant ship seized by Cambodia. If this defining Vietnam background is extended to include Cheney's prominent involvement in the 1991 Gulf War, it becomes clear that few regimes have chosen top defense strategy teams whose thinking has been so shaped by the experience of old wars and by an anxiousness to wipe away their lingering embarrassments.

—Kevin Phillips, *American Dynasty*
(New York: Viking Press, 2004), p.93

Dick & George

Q: What's the most valuable role Cheney plays for the President in White House activities on the war on terror?

RUMSFELD: First of all, I don't know that his role has changed since September 11th. It's hard for someone— It's hard for anyone other than the President and the Vice President to know precisely what role he plays. They are together for meals alone, they have meetings, they talk about things. They're very close. From my perspective it seems clear that they have an excellent relationship and that the Vice President plays the proper role of a vice president of an adviser, as opposed to a decider, if you will. The President's the decision maker and the Vice President is the person who has the background and the ability to listen to arguments on all sides and meet with the President and talk to him as a friend and as an adviser, as opposed to someone that is reporting to him in a statutory responsibility of some kind.

—Interview with Pam Hess,
United Press International, August 29/02

One of your tasks is to separate the "personal" from the substantive." The two can become confused, especially if someone rubs the president wrong.

—from "Rumsfeld's Rules"

Q: President Bush last night in Texas made it sound very personal, saying that Saddam is the person who is going after my dad, went after my dad. Is that part of the reason that we're going this course?

RUMSFELD: Oh, absolutely not. There's nothing personal about this at all.

—Interview with John Shirek,
WXIA Channel 11, Atlanta, September 27/02

Think how fortunate we are to have Dick Cheney serving as vice president. (Applause.) A superb executive, a wise counselor; the vice president is a combination of both thinker and doer. His quiet contributions will be well and properly recorded, not in the front pages of newspapers, but in the history books that are yet to be written. I am sure glad I discovered him! (Laughter.)

—Secretary Rumsfeld's remarks at the Hudson Institute's
presentation of the James Doolittle Award, May 13/03

"Cheney Says Peril of a Nuclear Iraq Justifies Attack," Powell read in *The New York Times*. . . . It was the lead story. . . .

—Woodward, *Bush at War*, p. 344

"It will only look bad if people raise the question . . ."

WILLIAMS: Trying to move smartly through my list: Corporate Responsibility—a division of Halliburton, a firm formerly headed by the vice president, Mr. Cheney, KBR has been given an enormous Pentagon contract, exclusive logistics supplier for both Army and Navy for cooking, construction, power generating, fuel transportation. The contract recently won from the Army is for ten years, has no lid on costs, the only logistical arrangement by the Army without an estimated cost. You know how it looks when the Pentagon awards an enormous contract to a company last headed by the current vice president. What is the Pentagon view on the selection of a vendor in this case?

RUMSFELD: Oh, I have no idea. I was not aware of the contract at all. There's, you know, hundreds of contracts in an institution as large as this, in all the services, and the defense agencies. I would say this. I think the implication of the question is unfair, in this sense—the vice president has absolutely no economic interest in any company that he was ever connected with. I have no economic interest. None of the other people serving in the government have an economic interest in any company they were previously associated with. Therefore, it ought not to look bad. It only will look bad if people raise the question, and say it looks bad. It does not look bad. And it should be accompanied by the truth, which is that the vice president has no economic interest in that company; has not since the day he became vice president.

—Interview with Brian Williams, CNBC, July 15, 2002

KROFT: Mr. Secretary, what do you say to people who think this is about oil?

RUMSFELD: Nonsense. It just isn't. There are certain things like that, myths, that are floating around. I'm glad you asked. It has nothing to do with oil, literally nothing to do with oil. It has nothing to do with the religion. People who have a viewpoint frequently throw up those two issues, and say, well, this is really against Muslims, which it certainly isn't. The United States is the country that went in and helped Kuwait, a Muslim country. We worked in Bosnia to stop ethnic cleansing. We've done Afghanistan. And it's certainly not about oil. Oil is fungible, and people who own it want to sell it, and it will be available.

—Interview with Steve Kroft,
Infinity Radio, November 14/02

On accommodation:

Bouncing on the balls of his feet at his lectern in the Pentagon's briefing room, Mr. Rumsfeld, who once did one-armed push-ups for cash as a Princeton student, is in his natural element. . . . If Iraqi paramilitaries wish "to die for Saddam Hussein," he says, "they will be accommodated."

—*The New York Times*, March 30/03

On relativity:

You folks are sitting here in one meeting. You're all going to go out and write something different. I don't know why you do that, but you will. You will all go out and write something that fits where you grew up, or what you thought when you came into this meeting, and what your personal perspective is, or what you think your editors want, or what you think your readers want. And you'll cherry-pick it. And I'll bet you if we took the stories out of this meeting, they would be all over the lot. That's the way countries are. That's the way people are.

—Roundtable with European journalists, February 6/04

DISCLAIMERS

I learned early on if you don't know, you say you don't know.

—Town Hall Meeting, Prince Sultan Air Base, April 29/03

If you don't know, I'm not going to tell you . . .

Q: Secretary Rumsfeld, were you a part of this decision to abandon Vieques or were you simply informed of it afterwards?

RUMSFELD: I have been in touch with Deputy Secretary Wolfowitz every day, several times a day on a whole host of subjects. So to suggest that anyone involved is not knowledgeable about it would be wrong.

Q: Well, what I'm asking is did you have input into this decision? Do you agree with it?

RUMSFELD: The decision has been handled, as I said, by Deputy Secretary Wolfowitz and by the secretary of the Navy, in whom I have great confidence, and I think they're handling it very, very well.

Q: Well, Mr. Secretary, we're asking your opinion as secretary of Defense. Can you share with us your specific thoughts on the decision made by these other individuals to leave Vieques? What—

RUMSFELD: I just said that I am in full agreement with the president of the United States, the deputy secretary of Defense and the secretary of the Navy. I don't know how anyone could be more explicit.

—Joint media availability at the Pentagon with Prime Minister Goh Chok Tong of Singapore, June 14/01

Musings . . .

Q: Mr. Secretary, you said that you have a lot of work to do to get the senior al Qaeda and senior Taliban still on the loose. What's your reaction to the release of seven Taliban leaders in Kandahar, and some of them senior?

RUMSFELD: I've read those reports and I've tracked them down two days in a row, and we can't verify that that ever happened, that there were ever those people in custody, that anyone—it's hard to be released if you were never in custody.

Q: So you're saying it didn't happen?

RUMSFELD: I'm not saying it didn't happen.

Q: Oh.

RUMSFELD: I'm saying precisely what I said.

Q: Okay.

RUMSFELD: That for two days, I've tried to track down these fascinating stories . . . and I am not able to do so. I find—I keep pursuing it and saying, "My goodness. They can't all be wrong. Please see if you can't find what they're writing about." And they come back to me with something like this; that it may be that there are some senior Taliban somewhere, not necessarily in any area or any country, but it may be that there are some, a handful, maybe even that right number, and it may be that one or more or them called and talked to some subordinate in one of the Taliban elements in Afghanistan and said, "Hey, there's a few of us around who might like to turn ourselves in if the deal was right, but we're not going to tell you where we are, and we want to see about how this might work." And it might be that that got reported up and rejected, and someone could say, "Gee, X number were in custody and released, because the deal was never made." Now, how many times is that going on in Afghanistan today? I would guess a dozen. . . . But I can't find what people have been writing about and talking about on television. I can't find it. But this does not say it didn't happen.

—DoD News Briefing, January 11/02

If I can help it, you'll never know . . .

Q: In regard to Iraq weapons of mass destruction and terrorists, is there any evidence to indicate that Iraq has attempted to or is willing to supply terrorists with weapons of mass destruction? Because there are reports that there is no evidence of a direct link between Baghdad and some of these terrorist organizations.

RUMSFELD: Reports that say that something hasn't happened are always interesting to me, because as we know, there are known knowns; there are things we know we know. We also know there are known unknowns; that is to say we know there are some things we do not know. But there are also unknown unknowns—the ones we don't know we don't know. And if one looks throughout the history of our country and other free countries, it is the latter category that tend to be the difficult ones.

—DoD News Briefing, February 12/02

I really don't like to talk about what other countries do . . .

Q: And could you, given the presence—the military presence that we now have off the coast of the Horn of Africa and renewed al Qaeda activity in that area, explain what the DoD policy is with regard to taking lethal action in countries? Is it only at the request or permission of the government, or is it only in places where there is no sovereign government in existence?

RUMSFELD: Those are very good questions.

Q: Thank you.

RUMSFELD: And I happen also to agree with you that a discussion of them at some point would be—

Q: I take it that would be not now? (Laughter.)

RUMSFELD: The—let me think how I can say this. Let's start with the beginning. I don't really like to talk about what other countries do or don't do. I really believe that it is in our country's interest to let them do that. Every country has different sensitivities. So about half of your questions—

Q: Well, I'm asking what the DoD policy is.

RUMSFELD: I'm working my way over to figuring out how I won't answer that. (Laughter.)

—DoD News Briefing, December 3/02

Being the kind of country we are . . .

Q: Mr. Secretary, you said, that for the most part, the detainees will be treated in a manner consistent with the Geneva Convention. Exactly which parts, which rights, privileges of the Geneva Convention will they have, and who will decide, and when will it be decided on an ad hoc basis? And just as a follow-up, can you say if there's been any—

RUMSFELD: Well, let me work on that one for a minute. That's a mouthful. What we've said from the beginning is that these are unlawful combatants in our view, and we're detaining them. We call them detainees, not prisoners of war. We call them detainees. We have said that, you know, being the kind of a country we are, it's our intention to recognize that there are certain standards that are generally appropriate for treating people who were—are prisoners of war, which these people are not, and—in our view—but there—and, you know, to the extent that it's reasonable, we will end up using roughly that standard. And that's what we're doing. I don't—I wouldn't want to say that I know in any instance where we would deviate from that or where we might exceed it. But I'm sure we'll probably be on both sides of it modestly.

—DoD News Briefing, January 11/02

Q: Mr. Secretary . . . I wanted to begin asking you about the situation on Guantanamo Bay and about the treatment of the detainees that have been brought over to Cuba. My first question is this. You have made a public commitment to humane treatment of these detainees.

RUMSFELD: Why my goodness yes. That's what our country does is treat people humanely.

Q: But how does that square with what we know of their condition, being kept in what are being described as cages, six foot by eight foot, the hoods and the shackles that we just caught a glimpse of as they were being put onto the planes in Kandahar. Many groups, both in the United States and outside, do not feel that that is humane treatment.

RUMSFELD: Well, I can't speak for many groups but I can assure you that the United States has been from the outset, is now, and will in the future treat all detainees in a humane way. What you have is a photograph taken of people in transit. And the fact of the matter is that a), you're beginning with people that are very dangerous . . . one of the ways of helping people from becoming more dangerous than they otherwise might be is by putting hoods over their heads. Now they were put on

their heads during the transport period. They are not perma-
nent, unlike the burkhas that were required in Afghanistan by
the Taliban and the al Qaeda.

—Roundtable with radio media,
AP, BBC, NPR, and VOA, January 15/02

Q: Mr. Secretary? Among those detainees are, if I am not mistaken, at least six who are not in fact captured on the battlefield but were taken in Bosnia. Do you believe that you have—
that the United States—and I don't think charges were
pending against them, and no charges have been brought
against them—do you feel that you have the right essentially
to pick up anyone anywhere in the world whom you believe to
be a terrorist and hold them indefinitely, without bringing
charges against them for as long as you want, regardless of
whether they are actually captured, quote, "on the battlefield"?

RUMSFELD: No. I'd like to say it my way, and it would be something like this: that I will leave it to the lawyers to answer the
question the way you cast it. And I will say this: There is no question but that the United States of America has every right—as
does ever other sovereign nation—to defend itself. There is no
way to defend against terrorism except finding terrorists. And to
do that you must go where they are. And that is what we are
doing. And they may be in Afghanistan, they may be in Pakistan—and we have some people who have been turned over to
us from countries other than Afghanistan. And we place them
where we can. And at the moment we are placing them for the
most part, some in the United States as you know, and some in
Guantanamo, and there are still some in Bagram, and there are
still some that we are looking at that we do not have in custody
in Afghanistan, and some we do not yet have in custody from
Pakistan, and may or may not decide to take. And I think to try
to make a blanket statement like your question suggested would
be a poor way for me to approach it. And I can tell you that I
think that there is not going to be a single cookie mold that will

be pressed down over this aggregation of people. But we do know that we don't want prisoners, we don't want detainees. What we want to do is to defend the American people and our friends and allies and our deployed forces. And to do that, you've simply got to go find people and detain them.

—DoD News Briefing, March 28/02

Q: Mr. Secretary, you've said that you reserve the right to hold the detainees until the end of the war. You've also said that there won't be a signing ceremony on the Missouri in this war.

RUMSFELD: Right.

Q: So what exactly is the end of the war? And are we talking about the war on terrorism or the conflict in Afghanistan?

RUMSFELD: Well, at the moment, we all know the conflict in Afghanistan is still going on, so we're not past our deadline or our due date. I don't know how to describe it, and I suppose that will be something that the president would make a judgment on, as to when it was over. I think the better way to look at it is not at that group of people in the aggregate, but as I've indicated, individually. And there may be individuals that tomorrow one will come to a conclusion that they're no longer a threat for whatever reason. And as I say, that's already happened; we've released people already. So, I think that the way I would characterize the end of the conflict is when we feel that there are not effective global terrorist networks functioning in the world that these people would be likely to go back to and begin again their terrorist activities.

—DoD News Briefing, March 28/02

Q: The Geneva Convention lays out a review process for individuals who have been picked up on a battlefield to determine whether or not they are POWs. And the presumption under the convention is that individuals picked up are in fact POWs.

Why have you summarily dismissed the possibility that some of these people should be held under those rules?

RUMSFELD: Why would you use the word summarily?

Q: Because not a single individual at Guantanamo has received an Article 5 hearing.

RUMSFELD: I don't know that that's true.

Q: That would be news to me.

RUMSFELD: I'm not a lawyer. What happened was that the White House made a decision that a), they would be treated as— They were characterized as enemy combatants, I think was the phrase.

Q: Right.

RUMSFELD: And in fact it was unlawful enemy combatants. Number one. Number two they said, however, we will treat them in [a manner that is] consistent with the Geneva Convention and they are being treated in a manner that is consistent with the Geneva Convention as though they would be prisoners of war. Now as I recall this question has come up before and my recollection is that there need to be, two or three people need to sit down and look and make a judgment. Is that the tribunal you're referring to?

Q: It's a formal process, actually.

RUMSFELD: Right. It's relatively informal but it's a process that's specified, as I understand it. Clearly this review would be of a kind with that and probably could be characterized as that.

Q: But not a single individual at Guantanamo has been now designated as a POW, so—

RUMSFELD: No, no. You're quite right. They have not. They have been designated unlawful enemy combatants.

—Meeting with the editorial board of the
Tampa Tribune and *St. Petersburg Times*, February 17/04

For your information:

Asked at a news conference in London today to explain Mr. Bremmer's planned role, Mr. Rumsfeld said, "I could, but I won't."

—*The New York Times*, May 3/03

Not to worry . . .

The Rumsfeld record reveals a leader who has both a keen sense of urgency and an instinct for quickly getting to the heart of a problem—both hallmarks of effective leadership. These qualities may sound like obvious virtues, but the fact is that many leaders take too much time identifying the problem and outlining possible responses. Those moments of hesitation can mean the difference between success and failure.

—Jeffrey A. Kramer, *The Rumsfeld Way* (New York: McGraw-Hill, 2002), p. 55

Q: Here in New York and around the nation we are on heightened alert. . . . What can you say to Americans who are worried . . . ?

A: Well, I think they can have confidence that the problem has been properly identified.

—Interview with Dick Brennan, WNYW, May 27/03

We have plans to do everything in the world that we can think of . . .

Q: What about Haiti? Is it just—is the U.S. military going to be doing anything in Haiti, since it's now seeming to get even worse?

RUMSFELD: I guess the way to respond to that is that, needless to say, everyone's hopeful that the situation, which tends to ebb and flow down there, will stay below a certain threshold and that there's—we have no plans to do anything. By that I don't mean we have no plans. Obviously, we have plans to do everything in the world that we can think of.

—DoD News Briefing, February 10/04

Q: . . . was President Aristide forced out of Haiti by the U.S. military?

RUMSFELD: . . .You said that Aristide was claiming he was abducted, or what was the wording?

Q: Virtually.

RUMSFELD: Virtually?

Q: He claimed he was virtually kidnapped and forced to leave—

RUMSFELD: I don't believe that's true that he is claiming that. I just don't know that that's the case. I'd be absolutely amazed if that were the case. There may be somebody saying that he's saying that, but I don't believe that.

—DoD News Briefing, March 1/04

Point of clarification:

Q: Mr. Secretary, this attack today seems to line up with the plan outlined in that document recovered from Hassan Ghul, the al Qaeda operative who was captured in Iraq.

RUMSFELD: It does.

Q: Do you—what do you think that document says about the current state of operations, terrorist operations in Iraq?

RUMSFELD: I don't know. I haven't read it. I don't know if it's authentic. People who have read it think it is, but I haven't read it. My friend Dick has read it. Why don't we ask Dick? (Laughter.) General? (Laughter continues.)

MYERS: Thank you, Mr. Secretary.

RUMSFELD: You know, authenticity is still being evaluated, okay? So with that caveat—and this is initial analysis . . .

Q: Do you think that letter was heading out to top leaders in Afghanistan or Pakistan, or—?

MYERS: I'm not going to—I don't want to discuss it anymore.

RUMSFELD: You know, given all the discussion about absolutely perfect precision in any—every single thing anyone might want to say, I would like to help General Myers and have—and correct what I said. He probably did not read the letter, because it was in Arabic.

MYERS: Good point.

RUMSFELD: I think he probably read a translation of that letter.

MYERS: Actually, I read a first translation, and the warning on the first translation was, you better wait for the second translation. (Laughs.) That because they'll—you know, the first one was done fairly quickly, and there are nuances . . .

RUMSFELD: So I don't want someone coming back and saying that we—that he read the original letter.

Q: You're going to be even more careful with your words now?

RUMSFELD: I've always been careful. I'm going to—(laughs)— I'm going to try to be more successful. (Laughter.)

—DoD News Briefing, February 10/04

I'm willing to flow forces in support of diplomacy . . .

Q: Mr. Secretary, the Navy said today that a sixth aircraft carrier, the *Nimitz*, will depart San Diego for the Gulf next week on a routine exchange, but the carrier that it's replacing could be kept a while. And the Air Force says that B-2 stealth bombers are preparing to leave in the coming days. Is this the final push in your massive military buildup near Iraq? And does this signal anything particular, that—these major weapons systems?

RUMSFELD: I think, Charlie, what it signals is the fact that as I've indicated, the president has asked us to flow forces in support of diplomacy. The diplomacy is still under way in the United Nations.

—Media availability with Afghan President
Hamid Karzai, February 27/03

But, in case you haven't noticed, diplomacy is for wimps.

This is diplomacy and I don't do diplomacy. You may have noticed.

—Town Hall Meeting, Qatar, April 28/03

The Axman Cometh

The Boss from Hell:

Regardless of how one views Rumsfeld's ultracompetitive, contentious style, there is no doubt that he was an effective, results-driven CEO. If his behavior went "over the top" at times, it was because he could not tolerate failure in any form.

—Kramer, *The Rumsfeld Way*, p. 75

You not only let someone who has not been obeying you go, you do it publicly so everyone knows that breaking the rules brings immediate punishment. . . .

—Rumsfeld quoted in *Fortune* magazine, April 21/80, in which he was celebrated as one of "America's Ten Toughest Bosses"

I have a problem personally. I work long hours and seven days a week, and I'll ask somebody to do something and I will be absolutely certain I asked them two and a half weeks ago and it will turn out it was two and a half or three days ago. I have a certain amount of impatience about things. I like to get things done.

—Interview with Tom Ricks and Bradley Graham
of *The Washington Post*, December 7/01

The iterative process at work.

. . . the atmosphere was generally one of deference to authority, especially by Franks to Rumsfeld. In another meeting, Rumsfeld said something and the president asked Franks, "Tommy, what do you think?"

"Sir, I think exactly what my secretary thinks, what he's ever thought, what he will ever think, or whatever he thought he might think."

—Woodward, *Bush at War*, p.251

RUMSFELD: —everything anyone reads about what I have said or thought or dealt with by way of General Franks has been wrong. We work together very, very closely. It is an iterative process.

—Interview with Tom Bowman, *Baltimore Sun*,
December 27/01

You had to be there.

RUMSFELD: . . . Colin was sitting next to me and the prime minister of Australia and the foreign minister of Australia, the defense minister of Australia and Rumsfeld and Powell, for the 50th Anniversary of ANZUS. This woman said, "Mr. Secretary," to me, "are you and Secretary Powell on different sides of the North Korean issue," or whatever it was. I thought here we go.

I said—you can get the transcript, it's very funny, and this is an enormous roomful of people. I said look, Secretary—he's sitting right here—Secretary Powell and I agree on every single issue that has ever been before this administration except for those instances where Colin's still learning.

—Interview with Evan Thomas, *Newsweek*, January 14/02

When it comes to the DARPA Futures Market, I know nothing . . .

Q: Should Admiral Poindexter keep his job, and what do you think about the fallout from [inaudible re: DARPA Futures Market]?

RUMSFELD: I cancelled it an hour after I read about it. I did so, unfortunately not with a great deal of knowledge because it was too soon. I cancelled it because it was clear that even if it happened to have been a brilliant idea, which I doubt, it would not have been able to function in the environment that it was created, so I cancelled it. And I hope to have a chance this weekend to read about it and learn more about it and see what I think of it and how it happened and whether it made sense or didn't make sense but it was pretty clear to me it ought to have been cancelled so I did so.

—Stakeout at the Senate, July 30/03

It can't be done . . .

HELMS: I wish you could be in the den of our home sometime when Don Rumsfeld is being interviewed by the press, how he can handle it. He makes in most cases, certainly a lot of them, regret that they asked the question the way they did. (Laughter.) It's a pleasure and delight to watch some of them in the press to try to twist a question so that they can get the wrong answer to the right question. They just don't get it. It can't be done.

There is no spin with this gentleman. He tells the truth. He always calls it as he sees it. And America is lucky to have him serving at such a critical time.

—Jesse Helms, remarks introducing Secretary Rumsfeld, at the
15th anniversary of the Jesse Helms Center, October 18/03

Let's trade shoes.

JAMIE MCINTYRE (from CNN)**:** A year ago you came here and you met a lot of resistance from U.S.-European allies who believed that the UN inspections in Iraq were working and they should be given more time and you argued against that. Now you come back a year later, the U.S. having not found the weapons in Iraq that it believed were there—not found them yet—do you come back with any more sympathy for the European viewpoint than you experienced when you came here a year ago?

RUMSFELD: The way you phrased the question is unfortunate. (Laughter.} And had I been in your shoes I would have phrased it much differently and probably much better. (Laughter.)

—Press Conference, Munich, February 6/04

THE RIGHT MAN
IN THE
RIGHT PLACE
AT THE
RIGHT TIME

Absent the events of September 11th, the Rumsfeld phenomenon would not have been born, and the Rumsfeld story might not have been written.

—Kramer, *The Rumsfeld Way*, p. 4

Too little, too late . . .

Rumsfeld: In May of 2001, we began the process of streamlining the way the department prepares war plans, reducing the time to develop plans and increasing the frequency at which the assumptions would be updated. I should add that for much of that period, most of the senior officials selected by the president had not been cleared or confirmed by the Senate . . .

GORTON: Mr. Secretary, on page 10 of your written statement, you express what I think is justified frustration in the extended period of time it took you to get a team in place with which to make these decisions. You list nine of your senior staff, the earliest of whom was confirmed on the 3rd of May 2001, and the last of whom, interestingly enough, an assistant secretary for international security policy, not until August 6th. And you say that the confirmation system—that kind of confirmation system and those delays just don't work in the 21st century. I can greatly sympathize with you on that, but you leave out one very important factor. When were those nine people nominated and actually sent to the Senate?

RUMSFELD: Well, I wasn't suggesting in this that I—in fact, I hope I phrased it more elegantly than you did. (Laughter.) My point here, I hope—my point, whether I made it well or not, my point is, not simply the Senate confirmation, but the clearance process, the entire process, finding them, putting them through the FBI, putting them through multiple ethics. It took weeks for people to fill out their ethics forms. It cost a fortune for some people to fill out their ethics form. Then you have to go from the one in the executive branch to the one in the United States Senate and have that filled out in different forms. Some of you may have been through this. It's an amazing process. And then some guy walks in and gives you a drug test. (Laughter.) It is not just the Senate, although the Senate can be a problem, with all respect. (Laughter.)

GORTON: Thank you. Thank you for that clarification. So in your view, it's the whole process.

RUMSFELD: Entirely, yes.

GORTON: From a new administration finding who they want, getting them through various clearances and then the Senate. But we don't know here how long the Senate part of that took in any one of these cases.

RUMSFELD: Well, I know. And I could give it to you if you're interested.

GORTON: I think I would be interested.

—Public Testimony Before 9/11 Panel, March 23/04

Off the record . . .

Q: Mr. Secretary, today's the 30th anniversary of the Watergate break-in. And on *CNN Today* there was—they were engaging in a discussion of Deep Throat, who Deep Throat might be. One viewer e-mailed in to CNN, suggesting that you were Deep Throat. (Laughter.) Any comment?

RUMSFELD: You really are scraping the bottom of the barrel. (Laughter.)

Q: But you don't deny it, sir? (Laughter.)

RUMSFELD: (Laughs.) Oh, that is wonderful. That is amusing. I'd heard every name in the world except—no, I was kind of busy running the economic stabilization program and was not really engaged in that process.

Q: I'll take that as a no.

Rumsfeld: (Laughs.) That's a safe assumption. I do not want the record to show that I even bothered to deny it, however.

—DoD Press Briefing, June 17/02

It's a gift.

Fortune often favors those that have the rare gift of being in the right place at the right time. Even rarer, however, is the knack of being somewhere else. Donald Rumsfeld possessed both.

—Robert T. Hartmann, *Palace Politics*
(New York: McGraw-Hill, 1980), p. 273

Your intellectual cul-de-sac happens to coincide precisely with my concurrence of grammar and semantics . . .

Q: . . . I'm in kind of an intellectual cul-de-sac on your opening statement, and I'm hoping you can lead me out of it. What you described in the Cuban missile crisis is essentially an intelligence failure that led the United States and the Soviet Union to the brink of war. The events of 9/11—9/11 possibly occurred because of an intelligence failure; might have been prevented had intelligence been acted upon differently. And what has been described so far is a lack of intelligence or, therefore, an intelligence failure with regard to what Iraq is doing and what Iraq has. So then at the same time, there is, you know, lots of talk—"we can't tell you everything that we know." . . . I'm sort of having a hard time reconciling all of this and not coming up with the flip answer that the reason that the United States is considering and possibly preparing to use force in Iraq is because of a massive intelligence failure. And we don't know what we don't know, so let's go do this.

RUMSFELD: I don't like the phrase "intelligence failure." And I purposely didn't use it with respect to the—I don't think I used it—with respect to the Cuban missile crisis. I wouldn't use it with respect to September 11th.

I think the point I like to make is that we're living in a big world, where these technologies and capabilities are spreading across the globe. And many more countries and many more terrorist networks are going to be able to get their hands on them, and are getting their hands on them. And that it's not possible to know everything that's going on in this globe—no matter how good you are, no matter how effective your intelligence gathering is. You can know a lot, and you can make good estimates and guesses, but there are—we have to accept that we're going to live in a world of little or no warning, a world of surprises if you're still surprised.

But if you know that those capabilities are out there, and you know you can't know exactly where they are, or exactly who has them, or exactly what method they may or may not use to attack you, then you ought not to be surprised. The only thing surprising to me is that people are surprised, because that's the nature of our world.

And the Cuban missile crisis, one can say, was an intelligence failure. Anyone with 20/20 hindsight can go back and say they failed to know that. And that's not inaccurate from a grammatical standpoint, or from a semantic standpoint. It is, however, I think, an unrealistic expectation to think that it's possible to know exactly what's going in the—on the minds of people, or whether they have intent, whether they necessarily have capability because they have very effective means of denial and deception. And it's constantly a moving target.

—DoD News Briefing, October 22/02

Armed and dangerous . . .

RUMSFELD: This is fantastic! I've got a laser pointer! (Laughter.) Holy mackerel!

Q: Is it lethal?

RUMSFELD: It's close! I'll just keep it right in my hand here. That's terrific.

—DoD News Briefing, November 27/01

Quiz for Paul O'Neill: Who's he talking about?

Q: . . . How would you rate the president as a student, as someone who basically had been a governor, he'd been a pilot in the Air National Guard, but for you as someone who's seasoned in these affairs, how would you rate him in terms of being aware and learning about this complicated new world?

RUMSFELD: I guess what I would say is that from the day I met him in the year 2000, months and months and months before the election, he was interested, probing, challenging positions, asking questions, and has consistently demonstrated an enormous interest in the subject. And as a result of that interest and that confidence and enormous knowledge of the subject, the team he works with—the vice president, the secretary of state, the national security adviser—and, we have a very good relationship and the reason is he is a superb leader. He is a person who has excellent instincts. He's intensely interested. He's decisive. And he's got courage.

—Interview with Mark Thompson,
Time magazine, December 14/01

When I took this job I had a visit with the president shortly thereafter, and we talked about the situation that a lot of people in the world had come to conclude that the United States was gun-shy. . . .

—Donald Rumsfeld, *Time* magazine, December 31/01

Q: [President Bush was] leaning forward. What was your reaction?

RUMSFELD: Oh, I just loved it. (Laughter.) To have a president who is decisive, who is an absolute blotter in terms of information, who puts structure into problems and forces discussion and ideas to be channeled in directions that are constructive is—and then to make a decision and stick with it and have power behind the decision, and clarity. It doesn't get complicated. These aren't 50-part decisions. The clarity that comes out of one of those meetings is refreshing.

—Interview with Dan Balz and Bob Woodward,
The Washington Post, January 9/02

***It's good to have someone who can speak for the president
—especially a man who is walking substance.***

MAZETTI: As Torie probably told you we're doing a cover story on the Vice President and his trip to the Middle East. Obviously he has a difficult diplomatic assignment in this trip. You've known him for quite awhile. Why do you think he's the right person for this job? 'This job' specifically the trip to the Middle East.

RUMSFELD: I guess it depends on what you think the trip to the Middle East is. But in this instance this is his first trip to the Middle East as vice president. It comes at a time when the Middle East is clearly in a degree of difficulty and there's a level of violence that is higher than the norm in that part of the world. He knows the leaders in the region well; has for some time. He brings with him the unambiguous weight of the president. His relationship with President Bush is so well known in the world that when he arrives he is without question speaking for the president of the United States and is able to meet in very small groups with the key leaders in the region and carry the message of the administration, of the president. He's also very good at it. He is a person who is approachable, people like him, and he is walking substance.

—Interview with Mark Mazetti,
U.S. News and World Report, March 13/02

Got my mojo working . . .

RUMSFELD: . . . I'd rather be right than fast. I wish it were possible to do everything at once. The procedures in this department start two years ago and then run, and the freight train comes down the track and it's filled way over there, and until it runs to the end, you can't see what's inside of it. And every time you try to reach in, it's like putting your hand in a gear box, because this depends on that, and this depended on that, and each piece depended on something else. And you think you're making a wise decision if you grab in the middle of it, but in fact, if all the layers that led to those things are not re-addressed back up, you end up with a situation that is kind of ad hoc; it is—it's a perfectly responsible, isolated decision, but if you make a series of them, they end up random; they don't end up with coherence. And so all of this appetite to kill this, or do that, or start this, my attitude is, look, we'll do it the best we can. And as I look back, I say to myself, "Not bad."

Q: Mr. Secretary, could I just ask one thing about Gitmo—

RUMSFELD: Oh, no, no. I love that ending. I— (Laughter). If you think I'm going to mess that one up, you're wrong! No, sir! I'm out of here.

—DoD News Briefing, May 1/02

Q: Regarding terrorism and weapons of mass destruction, you said something to the effect that the real situation is worse than the facts show. I wonder if you could tell us what is worse than is generally understood.

RUMSFELD: Sure. All of us in this business read intelligence information. And we read it daily and we think about it and it becomes, in our minds, essentially what exists. And that's wrong. It is not what exists.

—Press Conference at NATO Headquarters,
Brussels, Belgium, June 6/02

A little conceptual underpinning goes a long way.

Q: It sounds to me like you're saying the evidence is there, it's time for action.

RUMSFELD: I'm not saying anything like that. That's not my job. That's the President's job. That's the United Nations' job. That's the Congress's job. My job as Defense Secretary is not that at all. I'm just trying to add a little conceptual underpinning to the debate that's taking place.

—Media Roundtable with the BBC
and Voice of America, September 13/02

Q: What happens if Syria doesn't change their behavior?

RUMSFELD: Oh, that's above my pay grade. Those are the kinds of things that countries and presidents decide. That's broad national policy. I am a participant, but I am certainly not a decider.

—Interview on NBC *Meet the Press*
with Tim Russert, April 13/03

Why do I always have to explain things?

When the U.S. commits force, the task should be achievable and at an acceptable risk. It has to be something that the United States is truly capable of doing. We need to understand that we have limitations. There are some things that this country and other countries simply can't do. There should be clear goals both as to the purpose of the engagement and what would constitute success so we can know when our goals have been achieved. Decisions, in my view, ought not to be made by committees.

—DoD News Briefing, October 17/02

The president is also still learning . . .

The president desperately wanted a signed treaty with the Russians to reduce strategic nuclear weapons. . . . Rumsfeld flooded the principals with close to a dozen classified memos—often pejoratively called "Rummygrams" or "Snowflakes"—voicing objections. . . . Powell watched in wonderment as Rumsfeld delivered a series of requests: that the treaty not be legally binding, that it not specify numbers of nuclear weapons, that it have a clause that would allow the U.S. to withdraw at a moment's notice, that it provide flexibility, that it require verification, and that smaller tactical nuclear weapons be included.

If the Russians were now our friends, a new ally, Rumsfeld

argued, why did we need a treaty? What difference would a piece of paper make? Rumsfeld lost on all counts. . . .

—Woodward, *Bush at War*, pp. 326-7

Don't begin to think you're the President. You're not. The Constitution provides for only one.

—from "Rumsfeld's Rules"

How do we crystallize the problem for the president? Rumsfeld asked. He deemed it part of his responsibility to think on the president's behalf. We have to have the right thoughts, complete thoughts.

—Woodward, *Bush at War*, p. 26

I think of myself as the link between the commander in chief, the president of the United States who represents the people of the country on these issues and everything that happens out there.

—Interview with Ralph Kinney Bennett,
Readers Digest, January 23/02

It's Rummy's World—and we're just lucky to be living in it!

Men are likely to say that they admire the way he knows his mind and talks tough and straight, or the way he manages so deftly to keep the press in its place, or, in more general terms, what he has done and is doing for the country. Women, on the other hand, tend to express their feelings about him less specifically, saying that they find him to be a particularly attractive combination of good-looking and smart and sexy. Both descriptions, however, can basically be summed up in a word that has for a considerable period of time been deprived of public legitimacy.

The word is *manliness*.

—Decter, *Rumsfeld*, p. 213

US AND THEM

Don't divide the world into "them" and "us."

You'll be back to today's opponents for their help tomorrow.

—both from *Rumsfeld's Rules*

We trust Pakistan and Pakistan trusts us . . .

GUMBEL: I don't know if you just heard Richard Roth's report from Pakistan, but he noted that the foreign minister, while reiterating his pledge of support, says the U.S. could help its case by releasing evidence to convince skeptics of bin Laden's involvement. Does that make sense to you?

RUMSFELD: Well, let me say two things about that. First, the United States is approaching this in a measured and steady manner. We are gathering all the information that's appropriate and we are beginning the process of following the president's instructions, which are really literally the only way to deal with a problem of terrorism like this, which is a worldwide problem, and that is to go after terrorism at its roots. That means to deal with terrorists and deal with the countries that harbor terrorists. You have to do that, because there's no way to defend in a free society. Terrorism strikes at what we are. We are a free people. That's what we as a people are. And terrorism tries to deny that freedom. Now, does it make sense to begin releasing intelligence information? Of course not.

—Interview with Bryant Gumbel,
CBS-TV *Early Show*, September 18/01

Point of clarification concerning ravelment:

From time to time, I see references in the press to "the coalition"—singular. And let me reiterate that there is no single coalition in this effort. This campaign involves a number of flexible coalitions that will change and evolve as we proceed through the coming period . . . A month from now, I expect someone somewhere might report that a particular nation is not doing something or has stopped doing something, and the speculation could be "Is the coalition coming apart or unraveling?" Well, let me make clear: No single coalition has "raveled," therefore, it's unlikely to unravel.

—DoD News Briefing, October 18/02

**Don't worry, we will provide you
with all the facts you need . . .**

Q: What the administration is doing right now is essentially asking the American public to support a possible war with Iraq that could be extremely costly in terms of money, American lives, Iraqi civilians, environmental issues . . . why should we trust the administration on this, sight-unseen, with its intelligence? Because I understand that much of it won't be shared with us. There is a long tradition, and I think a very healthy one, of American people not trusting government but, rather, saying, prove it to us before you ask us to make this decision. And please don't say, you know, "It's either trust us or trust Saddam Hussein," because I don't think that's a fair decision— or a fair question to ask.

RUMSFELD: Did you think I was going to answer it that way?

Q: Actually, Wolfowitz did answer the question that way last week, Deputy Secretary Wolfowitz.

RUMSFELD: And he's not here to defend himself. (Laughter.) . . . Why should the American people trust their government, is the question, I guess. The—first of all, they don't have to trust their government blindly. The leaders have the responsibility to persuade, and persuasion means you marshal facts and you marshal argumentation, and the combination of the two results in persuasion.

—DoD News Briefing, January 29/03

They never really believed we had a monopoly on wisdom.

I think what you're seeing really is the fact that with the end of the Cold War, the threat from the Soviet Union gone, the countries of the world always were grateful to the United States for being the thing that kept expansionism from the Soviet Union from dominating other continents. But they never really believed we had a monopoly on cultural wisdom or economic wisdom or political wisdom. And with the end of that threat, why, people are a little freer to say what they think. And that's understandable. We can live in a world like that.

—Interview with Neil Cavuto, *Fox News*, July 20/01

Blessed are the peacemakers.

The United States has been a good citizen in the world, and interestingly, if one thinks about it, there are very few times in history where we've had a nation that happened to be the sole superpower on the face of the earth that coveted no one else's land, no one else's treasure, was willing through the good will of the American people to help to contribute to peace and stability in the world so that people can go about their lives and have their families and go to school and work and prosper.

—Interview with Karen Sauss,
KSDK-TV St. Louis, August 14/01

Doesn't pass the smell test . . .

In the early 1980s, Iran and Iraq were in a war. President Reagan was president, and I was a private citizen. 241 marines were killed in Beirut, Lebanon, in a terrorist attack. President Reagan and Secretary of State George Shultz asked me if I would take a leave of absence from my business and come in and assist them for a period of months with respect to the problems in the Middle East.

I met with Saddam Hussein during that period. And the purpose was to attempt to see if the Iraqi regime could be at all helpful in our efforts in the Middle East with respect to terrorism. In fact, I had nothing to do with helping Saddam Hussein and his regime against Iran. We had, I think, one or two meetings. The United States then did provide intelligence information, as I understand it—but I was back in private business at the time—to that regime.

—Secretary Rumsfeld media availability
in Qatar, December 11/02

There certainly is!

Q: Mr. Secretary, the Saudis were very public last week in saying they didn't want offensive strikes mounted from their bases. . . .

RUMSFELD: To the extent that nations are well knitted together at the top and have a good understanding and appreciation of the thinking of the senior people, those kinds of things get worked out. . . . These things don't tend to pose problems as long as there is a good strong relationship at the top and in this case there certainly is.

—Media availability at the Riyadh Conference
Palace Hotel, October 3/01

No guns for us . . .

We're an open country. We're a democratic country. Our borders with Canada are for all practical purposes, open. Our borders with Mexico are, for all practical purposes, open. We are quite open to people coming and going in our nation. We don't spend all of our time carrying pistols or rifles to defend ourselves. We expect the best of our fellow man. And when a group of people decide that we're wrong and we should not expect the best of our fellow man, then we have to consider what we do about that.

—Interview with Al Jazeera, October 16/01

Our little idiosyncrasy . . .

Q: Could you clarify something you said earlier? You said, with regard to capturing of these prisoners, "They will turn them over to us or they will not be positioned in places where they will come in contact with the people we would like to have." Does that mean that the folks that are fighting alongside the United States, whoever they are, over there, have formally agreed to hand them over to the U.S., or is this like the arrangement with the Afghans whereby everyone understands the personal force of General Franks and they're not likely to cross him?

RUMSFELD: Well, I—in my response, it was in the context of a question relating to the European Union's no death penalty position. And I was not referring to the Afghan forces on the ground. . . . So what did I mean? What I meant was that if a country has a sensitivity or a sensibility with respect to the death penalty, that's their privilege. We just don't want it to get in our way with respect to the people who fit in these senior-level categories. That means that either forces on the ground or—with whom we're cooperating or who might be involved in the security force in Kabul would understand that idiosyncrasy on our part. And they would agree either that they would not take control over people and turn them over to us, or we would agree that they would not be put in proximity where they might have occasion to take control over such people.

—DoD News Briefing, December 11/01

Guilty of firing in self-defense and not speaking English . . .

NPR: Each day this week the *Washington Post* has had another story on an accident, a raid, a bombing mission in which civilians in Afghanistan have been hit. Are . . . these the result of intelligence failures or is it a case of U.S. forces being used by rival Afghan factions to target one another?

RUMSFELD: . . . The other possibility is that everyone's right. That is to say that you go after a compound and in one building in a compound are people who are not Taliban or al Qaeda and next door are Taliban or al Qaeda, and the people coming in, the Special Forces entering the compound get fired on and the people who are the al Qaeda or Taliban fire on them so they return fire. They then don't know what is in the other house and it may turn out that there are innocents in the other house, that is to say non-Taliban, non-al Qaeda. So if somebody says that they were fired on and they were al Qaeda and Taliban, they're right. But if someone in the other house who isn't Taliban or al Qaeda says they were fired on and they weren't, they could also be right. So you could have one of those strange situations where everyone's right.

—Interview with Bob Edwards,
NPR *Morning Edition*, February 13/02

Q: Mr. Secretary, is the investigation complete into the January 24th raid at Hazar Qadam. Have you determined whether or not you killed and arrested people that you didn't intend to kill and arrest?

RUMSFELD: . . . I think it was January 23rd . . . at a place called Hazar Qadam—Q-A-D-A-M—there were two compounds. They were observed, we are told, over a period of several weeks. The signature and the intelligence information that was gathered over these several weeks were persuasive and compelling.

They used the word "signature"—it provided a signature, and a belief on the observers' part that there was al Qaeda or Taliban activity there. However, it was not strong enough to simply call in an airstrike, which would have been clearly the easiest, quickest thing to do. So they did not do that. Instead, they decided to go in and conduct a ground direct-action activity, which they did do.

And as they proceeded toward these two compounds, my information is that the people in one compound did not fire at them, and they entered the compound and captured a number of people. . . . As they approached the second compound . . . an individual saw them, went inside the compound, and shortly thereafter, the people inside the compound began firing at the U.S. Army forces that were moving toward that compound. In the course of the firefight, some number between 10 and 15, as I recall, of the Afghan people in that second compound were killed.

In that compound, and in the other compound, the Special Forces proceeded, and to the extent people did not resist, they were put in plastic cuffs and held. To the extent people did resist, they were subdued physically and put in plastic cuffs and held. They then were placed aboard helicopters and moved to some other location. Whether it was Kabul or Kandahar, I don't recall. And they were then interrogated, and after a period of some days, the individuals were released. I think that the way to characterize it is that there—it is—it appears to the people who reported to me that in fact these individuals were not Taliban or al Qaeda. . . .

—DoD News Briefing, February 21/02

Q: Mr. Secretary, I was in that very village three days after the raids—

RUMSFELD: Were you?

Q: And there seemed to be considerable discrepancies between what you're saying and what the locals reported in very large numbers, including the fact that it seems that U.S. forces had no interpreters with them; that the people in the building where 19 people were killed were shouting that "we're friends, we're friends" in Pashtu; that most of them were found dead in their beds; that there were considerable other discrepancies that don't match with what you're reporting here. Is there any intention to go further into this case, especially the fact that the building that was hit, where 19 people were reportedly killed, was in fact a collection point for weapons that were surrendered by the Taliban to people, we were told, associated with Mr. Karzai.

RUMSFELD: I've never heard or seen or watched an incident where there were not various reports and discrepancies about what happened. If you watch a car accident and ask five people standing on the street what took place, they will come up with different versions of what took place. We know that.

—DoD News Briefing, February 21/02

Q: I find it kind of odd that you say that they were shooting in self-defense, when in fact they were the ones who were—the Special Forces were the ones who were attacking in this incident. And also—

RUMSFELD: I'm trying to think what a better word would be.

—DoD News Briefing, February 21/02

My way or the highway . . .

I, as a student of history—we all know that in a number of periods of history, there have been—there's been almost unanimity in a certain position and it's proved to be wrong. So the fact that voices can cluster in a certain way does not mean that that is necessarily the wise course or the prudent course.

—DoD News Briefing, August 20/02

Q: Sir, a question about the mood among European allies. You were talking about the Islamic world a second ago. But now the European allies. If you look at, for example, France, Germany, also a lot of people in my own country—I'm from Dutch public TV, by the way—it seems that a lot of Europeans rather give the benefit of the doubt to Saddam Hussein than President George Bush. These are U.S. allies. What do you make of that? . . .

RUMSFELD: What do I think about it? Well, there isn't anyone alive who wouldn't prefer unanimity. I mean, you just always would like everyone to stand up and say, Way to go! That's the right thing to do, United States.

Now, we rarely find unanimity in the world. I was ambassador to NATO, and I—when we would go in and make a proposal, there wouldn't be unanimity. There wouldn't even be understanding. And we'd have to be persuasive. We'd have to show reasons. We'd have to—have to give rationales. We'd have to show facts. And, by golly, I found that Europe on any major issue is given—if there's leadership and if you're right, and if your facts are persuasive, Europe responds. And they always have.

Now, you're thinking of Europe as Germany and France. I don't. I think that's old Europe. If you look at the entire NATO Europe today, the center of gravity is shifting to the east. And there are a lot of new members. And if you just take the list of all the members of NATO and all of those who have been invited in recently—what is it? Twenty-six, something like that?—you're right. Germany has been a problem, and France has been a problem.

—DoD News Briefing, January 22/03

Point of clarification:

I'm told that when I used the phrase "old Europe" the other day, it caused a bit of a stir. I don't quite understand what the fuss is about. As I said at the time—at my age, I consider "old" a term of endearment. Like an old friend.

—Address to the Munich Conference on
European Security Policy in Munich, Germany, February 8/03

Q: Nick Phase of BBC. You're the author of the most famous and notorious remark for Europeans at least that when you divided Europe into old Europe and new Europe. I wonder since some months have passed if you'd like to say if you stick by this remark or if you'd like to modify it or you'd like to retract it?

RUMSFELD: None of the above.

—Remarks at the Eisenhower National
Security Conference, September 25/03

Our story has a life of its own . . .

Cornelius: Mr. Secretary, I guess the major reason for that reluctance on the European side, especially on the German side, is based on the fact that there seems to be a confusion in the goals the U.S. actually is trying to achieve in the Iraq case. The reasoning went from anti-terrorism to disarmament of weapons of mass destruction to regime change to fighting a dictatorship to human rights issues to energy supply and to terrorism, reforming the Middle East, setting up a beacon of democracy or a pseudo democracy, whatever, a stable regime to shine in that region. What is it actually for?

RUMSFELD: That's a clever question. It also is inaccurate. To say that it's gone from this to this to this to this is not correct.

—Question and answer session in
Munich, Germany, February 8/03

As I've said many times, there is no need to reinstitute the draft.

SCHIEFFER: Let me ask you about a criticism that's been leveled by the Military Officer's Association of America, that's 300,000 retired and active duty officers, who say that your plan to increase the size of the Army by the policy they call stop loss is simply a back door way to reinstitute the draft. They say that when you decided to increase the force levels up to, I think, 30,000 . . . instead of doing that by recruiting more people, what you've doing is telling people who are already in the service that they're going to have to stay an extra amount of time, maybe as much as 16 months. And what they say, this is their criticism, is this is the most unfair kind of draft, because what you're doing is drafting people who have already served the country. What is your response to that?

RUMSFELD: Well, obviously, they're not well informed. . . . The plan for the Army is not my plan for the Army, it's the Army's plan for the Army. General Schoomaker and Lee Brownlee have put it forward, they've testified on it. And we have been increasing the size of the Army for close to two years. We have emergency power to do that, we've been doing that.

SCHIEFFER: You're not saying, sir, are you, that this is not what they're doing?

RUMSFELD: I am saying that's not what they're doing. I'm saying—I don't know the full statement that you're referring to, but let me just tell you what's happening . . . what is happening is, the Army is going from something like 33 brigades up to 43 or 48 brigades over the next four years. We are rebalancing our Guard and Reserve with the active force, because we inherited a badly imbalanced, unbalanced Army, as between the skill sets in the active force and the Guard and Reserve. And the progress that General Schoomaker has been making is impressive.

Second, the suggestion that—stop loss has always been used. And it is not used excessively today. Everyone bends over backwards not to use it.

SCHEIFFER: But, are you using it now?

RUMSFELD: Just a minute. Everyone in the service who is there is a volunteer. And the idea of equating that to conscription, or a draft is inaccurate, and misses the point entirely. Everyone there is a volunteer.

SCHEIFFER: Yes, sir, but they volunteer for a certain period of time, and then when they're told, as they're about to get out, that they're going to have to stay longer—

RUMSFELD: Bob, you're wrong. They volunteer—

SCHEIFFER: This is not my thing, this is what the Military Officer's Association of America is saying.

RUMSFELD: I am telling you that the fact is that everyone serving on active duty is a volunteer, and they volunteered knowing precisely what the rules were. And they've known that stop loss has been a part of that policy or rule throughout a very long period of time. It's nothing new.

SCHEIFFER: Do you know how many people have been affected by stop loss, say, in the last couple of years?

RUMSFELD: We do. I don't have it on the tip of my tongue, but that number—

SCHEIFFER: Would it be about 30,000?

RUMSFELD: Over time, over some period, like a day, or a week, or a month, that someone may have served somewhat longer, that number might be right. I don't know.

—Interview with Bob Schieffer and Tom Friedman,
Face the Nation, CBS-TV, March 14/04

THE PERILS OF
CATASTROPHIC SUCCESS

Q: Was there some misjudgment in the number of people needed, the resources needed to get Iraq back on its feet following the heaviest fighting?

A: I don't believe so, I think there was an expectation that we could have what we did have, mainly very rapid success, and the military planned for that, they called it catastrophic success. In other words at some moment you could win before you anticipate it.

—Interview with Todd McDermott, WCBS TV, May 27/03

Like any calculating strategist [Rumsfeld] was always planning his next move. This has been a Rumsfeld constant throughout his career: for example, five days after the terrorist attacks, in planning sessions with the president and his team, Rumsfeld remarked: "This is chess, not checkers. We must be thinking beyond the first move." So even before the U.S. had implemented step one, Rumsfeld was anticipating the next three or four moves down the line.

—Kramer, *The Rumsfeld Way*, p. 82

Museums are for wimps.

Q: Mr. Secretary, as impressive as the U.S. military operation has been, no military plan is perfect. Would you concede in retrospect that perhaps the plan failed to adequately protect Iraq's antiquities, particularly the looting, providing enough security for the museum in Baghdad?

RUMSFELD: Looting is an unfortunate thing. Human beings are not perfect. We've seen looting in this country. We've seen riots at soccer games in various countries around the world. We've seen destruction after athletic events in our own country. No one likes it. No one allows it. It happens, and it's unfortunate. And to the extent it can be stopped, it should be stopped. To the extent it happens in a war zone, it's difficult to stop.

The United States is concerned about the museum in Baghdad, and the President and the Secretary of the State and I have all talked about it, and we are in the process of offering rewards for people who will bring things back or to assist us in finding where those things might be. And I would suspect that over time, we'll find that a number of things were in fact hidden prior to the conflict. That's what most people . . . who run museums do prior to a conflict, which was obviously well telegraphed in advance. But to try to lay off the fact of that unfortunate activity on a defect in a war plan—it strikes me as a stretch.

Q: But weren't you urged specifically by scholars and others about the danger to that museum? And weren't you urged to provide a greater level of protection and security in the initial phases of the operation?

RUMSFELD: Not to my knowledge.

—DoD News Briefing, April 15/03

Q: Mr. Secretary, given the intimacy of your own involvement in the planning of this war, what role did you have in the decision to protect the Oil Ministry but not the hospitals and not the national museum of Baghdad? . . .

RUMSFELD: With respect to the question, the question assumes that such a decision was made. And I think that premise is very likely inaccurate.

—Joint media availability with Geoffrey Hoon, May 2/03

Never-ending kinetics . . .

You'll recall that when President Bush indicated that the major military activities had ended we said very explicitly that he did not mean that the—that was the end of kinetics; that there would continue to be significant efforts to root out the remnants of the regime.

—DoD News Briefing, June 18/03

I have delegated the thinking-ahead part.

Q: General Garner suggested also that some very simple— seemingly simple measures although they may not have been that simple to execute could have made a difference. Installing a cell phone network immediately, bringing large generators to Baghdad immediately, that the entire situation in Iraq might be different had you taken those small steps?

RUMSFELD: Well General Garner was in charge of that process—the ORHA and he did a great many things that were enormously helpful. I don't think anyone anticipated the futility of the Baghdad power system.

—Interview with Steve Inskeep,
NPR *Morning Edition*, August 18/03

STEPHANOPOULOS: What wasn't foreseen?

RUMSFELD: Well, one of the things that wasn't foreseen is the extent to which the Iraqi infrastructure was degraded over the decades of his dictatorship. It was more decrepit, if you will, the oil infrastructure, the electrical grid, those types of things. So it took somewhat longer to get them up to speed than had been anticipated.

—Interview on ABC *This Week* with
George Stephanopoulos, November 2/03

LESSONS LEARNED

The Department of Defense always does a Lessons Learned exercise after a conflict and it's a good thing to do.

—Interview with Todd McDermott, CBS-TV, May 27/03

First we must deceive ourselves . . .

We have to be willing to face reality. You know, I have always believed if you begin with the truth, if you begin with reality— you can argue about opinion, you can argue about policy, but if you're arguing about facts, you're in trouble. And when people politicize facts, because they don't like them, they disserve the American people and they disserve the people of Europe and the people of Asia.

—Media availability en route to Ankara, Turkey, June 3/01

Truth is beauty . . .

Q: Mr. Secretary, how do you respond to people who are saying that the fact that Omar and bin Laden remain at large and their whereabouts—the United States apparently having no clue as to their whereabouts is making—beginning to make the United States look ineffective and at a loss?

RUMSFELD: Well, you know, something's neither good nor bad, but thinking makes it so, I suppose, Shakespeare said.

—DoD News Briefing, January 3/02

Small is beautiful.

We do need to be quicker on our feet. We need to be able to do things in hours and days instead of weeks and months. We need to be able to do things with somewhat smaller footprints.

—Town Hall Meeting, Qatar, April 28/03

We are not prepared to rule things out . . .

The United States governments, in successive administrations of both political parties, over my lifetime, which is pretty long, has never tended—has never really leapt up and ruled things out. It's not a helpful thing to do.

—Interview with Tony Snow on *Fox News Sunday*, May 4/03

RUMSFELD: The proposal that we've made is precisely what I said. It is to permit the study of less than 5 kiloton weapons.

Q: Okay. What would that kind of weapon possibly in the arsenal be used for?

RUMSFELD: We don't know. That's why we want to study it. And we're kind of inclined to think that the idea that we should not be allowed to study such a weapon is not a good idea.

—DoD News Briefing May 30/03

These people are like children . . .

Q: How long do you expect that an international presence will be necessary in Afghanistan and in Iraq?

RUMSFELD: You always just hope and pray that it won't be long. It is such an unnatural thing. And you also hope and pray that you have the patience and the good judgment to have it be long enough—so you don't do all of that and then have it fail. It is like when you teach your youngster how to ride a bike, and you put your hand on the back of the seat and you run down the street, and you know if you let go they might fall, but if you don't let go you have a four-year-old that can't ride a bike.

—Roundtable with European journalists, February 6/04

We need to be quicker on our feet . . .

SCHIEFFER: . . . David Kay said last week that the president should simply come clean with the American people. He said . . . the president should say we were simply mistaken, and that we're determined to find out why. And he said until we say that, it's going to hurt American credibility and delay reforms in intelligence, which simply need to be done.

RUMSFELD: Well, I didn't see the full statement that he made, but I would say this about that: First of all, there are lessons being learned about intelligence, and the Central Intelligence Agency, and the intelligence community have engaged in a lessons learned process. And there isn't any delay, as that statement suggests in addressing those issues, to the extent they're known at this point.

Second, David Kay . . . indicated that he thought we knew about 85% of what we'd know. . . . And I think it's perfectly proper to reserve final judgment until we've been able to go through that process, run down those leads and see what actually took place.

The president has said, essentially, what David Kay said, that thus far we know what's been delivered, and what's been discussed publicly, and we suspect there's more to be learned. And that's why we're spending so much time and effort interrogating people. There are millions of documents yet to be reviewed, literally millions of documents.

—Interview with Bob Schieffer and Tom Friedman,
Face the Nation, CBS-TV, March 14/04

It's easier to get into something than to get out of it.

You will launch many projects, but have time to finish only a few.

—both from "Rumsfeld's Rules"

SIZE MATTERS

Q: You say you're running out of targets [in Afghanistan] . . . What are you going to continue to hit?

RUMSFELD: Well, for one thing, we're finding that some of the targets we hit need to be re-hit. Second, we're not running out of targets, Afghanistan is. (Laughter.)

—DoD News Briefing, October 9/01

You didn't read the fine print . . .

Q: Mr. Secretary, about the reward, the question you hear all the time is what is an Afghanistan person going to do with $25 million?

RUMSFELD: Well it is not necessarily $25 million, it is up to.

—Media availability en route to
Fort Bragg, N.C., November 21/01

It costs a lot—but we're it . . .

LEHRER: But as a practical matter, Mr. Secretary, Tom Friedman of *The New York Times* pointed this out in his column yesterday, that we're it as far as high-tech weaponry, as far as air power is concerned. Our budget, this budget if it goes through will be equal to the next 16 countries combined in terms of what they spend on military. I mean we're pretty much it when it comes to major military operations, are we not?

RUMSFELD: That is true. We have "the" greatest capability. On the other hand, we can't and don't function alone. We have wonderful cooperation from literally dozens and dozens of nations in the war on terrorism. We're sharing intelligence. We don't have a monopoly on intelligence. We do have certain things. We do have more high-tech weapons, that's true. We do have more airlift, that's true. But the cooperation we get is enormously valuable to us.

> —Interview with Jim Lehrer,
> PBS "Newsmaker," February 4/02

With God on our side . . .

The Rumsfeld who became America's twenty-first secretary of defense in January, 2001 was well prepared for the tasks that would fall to him. He was technically skilled, having run the Byzantine bureaucracy of the White House staff and . . . he was also *morally grounded* [author's emphasis], and surprisingly willing to discuss complex issues in moral terms.

For example, he sees America's war on terrorism as a "moral war"—a conflict that for moral reasons we have no choice but to fight. In taking on the Taliban and Al Qaeda . . . he believes he is acting as a moral agent. . . . While it may sound simplistic, to Rumsfeld, America's battle against terrorism is a case of good versus evil.

> —Kramer, *The Rumsfeld Way*, p. 116

RUSSERT: There are many in the world asking for more time for negotiations, for diplomacy—the Vatican—the pope issued this statement: "Whoever decides that all peaceful means available under international law are exhausted assumes a grave responsibility before God, his own conscience and history."

RUMSFELD: It's true.

RUSSERT: And you accept that?

RUMSFELD: Indeed. It is a fair statement.

> —Interview on NBC *Meet The Press*
> with Tim Russert, March 23/03

Our God is bigger than theirs . . .

The Pentagon has assigned the task of tracking down and eliminating Osama bin Laden, Saddam Hussein and other high-profile targets to an Army general who sees the war on terrorism as a clash between Judeo-Christian values and Satan.

Lt. Gen. William G. "Jerry" Boykin, the new deputy undersecretary of Defense for intelligence, is a much-decorated and twice-wounded veteran of covert military operations. From the bloody 1993 clash with Muslim warlords in Somalia chronicled in "Black Hawk Down" and the hunt for Colombian drug czar Pablo Escobar to the ill-fated attempt to rescue American hostages in Iran in 1980, Boykin was in the thick of things.

Yet the former commander and 13-year veteran of the Army's top-secret Delta Force is also an outspoken evangelical Christian who appeared in dress uniform and polished jump boots before a religious group in Oregon in June to declare that radical Islamists hated the United States "because we're a Christian nation, because our foundation and our roots are Judeo-Christian . . . and the enemy is a guy named Satan."

Discussing the battle against a Muslim warlord in Somalia, Boykin told another audience, "I knew my God was bigger than his. I knew that my God was a real God and his was an idol."

"We in the army of God, in the house of God, kingdom of God have been raised for such a time as this," Boykin said last year.

On at least one occasion, in Sandy, Ore., in June, Boykin said of President Bush: "He's in the White House because God put him there."

—Roger T. Cooper, *Los Angeles Times*, October 16/03

STEPHANOPOULOS: It's also difficult to carry this on if we're giving the impression that this is somehow a war against a religion. Of course, you and the president have said you don't want to do that. But this was brought to the fore because of the controversy over General William Boykin. Have you had a chance yet to review his statements?

RUMSFELD: I have. I've seen what—first of all, there's no transcript of it, there's no video of it. There's a video of portions where people have written words underneath it. That's what I've been able to see. He does not have a tape or a transcript that one could see. And clearly, he has his views and they don't conform to the president's or mine. We do not believe this is a war against a religion. And I don't know that he does believe that. But he's a fine officer and we have an Inspector General reviewing the matter at the present time.

—Interview on ABC *This Week* with George Stephanopoulos, November 2/03

Countries can do anything they want—
as long as they are us . . .

Q: Am I right in thinking that you deliberately want us to believe that you are not disappointed with the degree [to which] some NATO members did or did not help you in Iraq?

RUMSFELD: I don't know that—first of all, any conclusion that I am deliberately trying to lead you to believe something is wrong. I am answering questions exactly the way they're being asked. My attitude about life is simple. I think countries ought to do what they want. I really do. It is up to them. Every country is different. They are sovereign and [inaudible].

Q: Is there nothing that binds you as a country in an international system? A legal framework or code of conduct?

RUMSFELD: I honestly believe that every country ought to do what it wants to do, and it has to live with the consequences. It either is proud of itself afterwards, or it is less proud of itself. Every country has a different history. They have a different perspective. They have a different political situation. They may be in a very fragile political circumstance at some moment. And we're all human beings, and we all make our own decisions. And does it bother me? No. I get up in the morning and take the world as I find it.

—Roundtable with European journalists, February 6/04

Q: Well, in the end, whether it's—even though it's Iraq's responsibility to comply with it and to prove that they've complied, in the end, won't it be the United States that judges whether Iraq is in compliance?

RUMSFELD: I think that certainly the United States would have an opinion. I also suspect that other countries in the United Nations, particularly the Security Council, will have opinions. And I don't know if they'll all agree.

Q: But they don't have to agree for the United States to take action it deems necessary, do they?

RUMSFELD: They don't have to—everyone does not have to agree for any member country to take appropriate action.

Q: So in the end, it will be the U.S. that decides?

RUMSFELD: Or any other country.

—DoD News Briefing, December 3/02

WEAPONIZING SPACE

What happens when a Determined Warrior takes unpopular positions? First, he generates opposition, even enemies—which at Rumsfeld's stage of life may not be a consequential consideration. Second, he generates debate, which Rumsfeld surely welcomes. (There will be no NMD without a spirited debate of its pros and cons.) And finally—and perhaps incidentally—he generates opportunities.

—Kramer, *The Rumsfeld Way*, p.193

Donald Rumsfeld chaired not one, but two, major advisory panels. . . . The second Rumsfeld panel, known as the Commission to Assess United States National Security Management and Organization . . . warns that the United States may someday soon face a "Space Pearl Harbor"—that is, a devastating sneak attack against U.S. satellites orbiting the planet.

Space warfare, the commission argues, has become "a virtual certainty": "We know from history that every medium—air, land, and sea—has seen conflict. Reality indicates that space will be no different." The report urges American leaders to reduce the country's vulnerability by developing "superior space capabilities," including the ability to "negate the hostile use of space against U.S. interests." This would require "power projection in, from, and through space."

—Michael Krepon, *Foreign Affairs*, May/June/01, p. 2

Q: But Mr. Secretary, as you look at the broad array of issues you're working on, the radical transformation you've described, personnel, weapon systems, etc., do you feel today that the billions required to research, test, develop and deploy missile defense is worth taking money away from all the other things that this department has to do every day, which most people believe is a more immediate threat to American national security?

RUMSFELD: Well I'm not in a position to have the knowledge that you've expressed in your question that most people think.

—Interview at the Pentagon with
a group of reporters, July 11/01

THE QUINTESSENCE
OF RUMMYISM

We have a choice, either to change the way we live, which is unacceptable, or to change the way that they live, and we have—we chose the latter.

—DoD News Briefing, September 18/01

The only defense against terrorism is offense.

—Town Hall Meeting at Nellis Air Force Base, February 20/02

You can start out with a perfectly plausible premise that's flawed but plausible, then proceed perfectly logically to a flawed conclusion. And the other thing that is always a risk in something like this is grabbing an argument of convenience because it's supportive and helpful and attractive early on, but down the road it becomes a burden because it was the premise for what you were doing and it garnered support, but it doesn't stand the test of time. Then pretty soon your support withers away.

—Interview with Georgie Anne Geyer, Universal Press Syndicate, October 17/01

RUSSERT: Let me turn to your memo of October 16th which has been leaked and share it with our viewers and ask you to talk about it: "With respect to global terrorism, the record since September 11th seems to be: We are having mixed results with al Qaeda. Today, we lack metrics to know if we are winning or losing the global war on terror. Are we capturing, killing or deterring and dissuading more terrorists every day than the madrassas, the schools, and the radical clerics are recruiting, training and deploying against us? It is pretty clear that the coalition can win in Afghanistan and Iraq in one way or another, but it will be a long, hard slog." Don't know if we are winning or losing?

RUMSFELD: Let me explain that. It's not that we don't know if we are winning or losing in Iraq or Afghanistan. We know what's happening there. The point I was making is this: if there are 90 nations engaged in the global war on terrorism, and if they are out arresting, capturing, killing terrorists, if they are out there putting pressure on their bank accounts, making it harder for them to raise money, making it harder for them to transfer money, making it harder for terrorists to move across borders, all of which is true, good progress is being made.

The question is that I posed—and I don't know the answer—is how many new terrorists are being made. . . .

—Interview on NBC *Meet The Press*
with Tim Russert, November 2/03

I know in my heart and my brain that America ain't what's wrong with the world.

—Munich Conference on Security Policy, February 7/04

This country cannot afford amateur hour in the White House.

—from "Rumsfeld's Rules"

A Final Question

LAMB: I noticed a couple of years ago that you quoted Alexis de Tocqueville in something that you were writing about. It leads me to a question, kind of a final question. Do you have a philosopher? Do you have someone that you follow over time as you've been a student in your life? Is there somebody in particular that you read?

RUMSFELD: Well, you can't be in this business and not be attentive to people like Sun Tzu and Clausewitz. I read history, mostly American history, but the philosophy certainly goes back to the founders of this country, as far as I'm concerned. I mean, the statement by Thomas Jefferson, "Here, sir, the people govern," is true. The American people have a system that they can affect, a process that they can affect. And it is going to be as good as they want or as poor as they're willing to allow. And their attentiveness, it seems to me, is critically important. And it's particularly important in a world that moves so fast, where things happen fast and where weapons are powerful and where mistakes can be serious.

I don't know what we teach in our schools that helps sensitize people to that, but it is amazing how we seem to do pretty darn well as a country. If the pendulum starts to move too far, people get out of their chairs and they seem to do what is necessary to push that pendulum back where it belongs. And it's a great testimony to the founders of the country.

—American Profile Interview with Brian Lamb
on C-SPAN TV, July 22/ 01